DEDICATION

➤ ⬅

I want to dedicate this work to all that have been sexually victimized by sexually dysfunctional men/women who believe it or not, are victims themselves, held against their will by the ultimate slave master, Satan himself. Many may argue that a Christian book so sexually explicit is too much and unnecessary, but for those that have been a slave of sexual perversions, you may understand. To those who've been taken advantage of sexually, God has heard your cry and your voice will be silenced no more. I put my voice behind yours and say #MeToo. God bless you!

~ Pastor Albert Amara

WELCOME!

SO GLAD YOU'RE HERE

"Aaahh!!! Not another book on sex, enough of that already!" someone would exclaim. But the answer is an emphatic, *yes*! In the wake of the sexual misconduct that shook America's political, corporate, and entertainment world starting with powerful men in Hollywood in October 2017, God told me after the first case broke that more men that used their positions to prey on the vulnerable will be exposed. Since that Word of the Lord to me, the stream of big names exposed seems full of water, as every week sponsors cut ties with a public figure, because of past sexual misconduct. I'm not writing this book because of what's happening in Hollywood or any other area of government, but because God told me to. He knew what was happening under cover and He wants to deliver people from the sexual bondage many are entangled in.

Please be advised that this is a Christian book about sexual purity, so there'll be lots of mention of sex, but it's not in a bid to be raunchy or salacious; rather, it is to expose the tricks of our enemy, Satan, and how to overcome them. Sometimes, we act as if admonitions on sexual inappropriateness are pesky little issues we need to be silent about, while we talk about the more important subjects. But, if we don't address this issue, we'll keep on repeating the same mistakes our leaders made and then pass it on to our children. This is a key cornerstone we cannot avoid having in the climbing of any mountain of success. Just today, November 29, 2017 as this book goes into production, I was watching the *700 Club* and overheard Pat Robertson talk of a lady that used to work on the old version

THE UNDEFILED
Bed

DELIVERANCE FROM SEXUAL BONDAGE

ALBERT AMARA

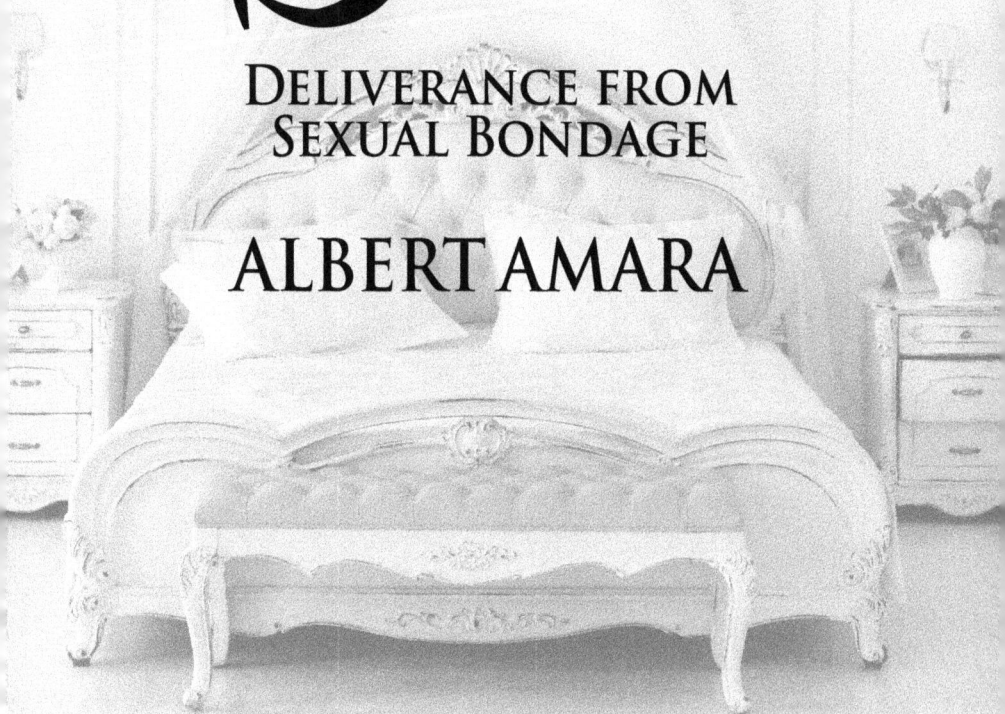

THE UNDEFILED
Bed

DELIVERANCE FROM
SEXUAL BONDAGE

ALBERT AMARA

HUNTER ENTERTAINMENT NETWORK

Colorado Springs, Colorado

Hunter Entertainment Network
4164 Austin Bluffs Parkway, Suite 214
Colorado Springs, Colorado 80918
www.hunter-ent-net.com
Tel. (253) 906-2160 – Fax: (719) 528-6359
E-mail: contact@hunter-entertainment.com
Or reach us on Facebook at: Hunter Entertainment Network
"Offering God's Heart to a Dying World"

This book and all other Hunter Entertainment Network™, Hunter Heart Publishing™, and Hunter Heart Kids™ books are available at Christian bookstores and distributors worldwide.

Chief Editor: Gord Dormer
Book cover design: Phil Coles Independent Design
Layout & logos: Exousia Marketing Group www.exousiamg.com

ISBN: 978-1937741-25-9

Printed in the United States of America.

of the *Hawaii Five O* show and she said as female staff members, they were expected to provide sexual favors for guests that came on the show. I believe God has seen all of these evil practices and is putting an end to and exposing all of these.

This used to be standard practice in Hollywood and other establishments that preyed on the vulnerable, but God's saying "enough is enough." I know women have their infidelities as well, but for the most part, men have been the offenders by a great majority. This book is not limited to men only, so if you're a woman struggling with sexual issues, this is for you, as well. The Holy Spirit has directed me not to be judgmental of one's weakness, as I was in your situation at one time. Paul said, "I was the chief of all sinners," but he was saved by the grace of God; this tells me that the grace of God is bigger than your sin. If the Lord brought me out, he can bring you out, as well.

Some may ask, "Why does this book focus on sex rather than the whole family?" To that I'll say God gave me a revelation on "The Undefiled Bed," because He knows many beds are defiled and He wants to clean it up before He can trust us with His power and His glory, which is coming to this earth before He comes back a second time. There are many books on success and wealth acquisition, but few on character and integrity, and the result is what's happening in the entertainment, political, business, and other sectors in our nation. It's time to adhere to the words of our Lord Jesus Christ in Matthew 7:24-27 and build strong foundations; foundations built on the rock called Christ, instead of sand. As we have seen lately, the men/women caught up in sex scandals are not some junkies on the street, but respectable people in suits with a raging sexual beast inside them.

Lastly, some of us are too embarrassed to discuss this subject in our churches, because we feel it's too private and may turn people off. While it's true sex is a private subject, I believe if there's any place it should be discussed it is in our churches. When you read God's Word, you'll find out He's not scared to talk about sex. In Song of Songs and Proverbs, He talks of romance. In Ezekiel, He spoke of His bride Israel lusting after Egyptians whose genitals were like those of donkeys and whose emission were like that of horses; this is God speaking and no one is holier than Him. My point is whether in private home cells, youth groups, or Bible studies, this needs to be addressed because every couple of months, we hear of a beloved saint of God caught in a sexual scandal. In our public schools, the government's gradually winning the minds of our children in issues like sex change, abortion with parental consent, and other sexual issues. Please approach and read this book with an open mind and the Holy Spirit will speak to you. Thank you for reading to the end! ~Albert

Hebrews 13:4

Marriage *is* honorable among all, and the
bed undefiled; but fornicators and
adulterers God will judge.

"The safest condom is the wedding ring as long
as the activity is practiced within the confines of
the marriage bed." ~ Albert Amara

"God will NEVER allow the counterfeit to
be better than the covenant." ~ Rebecca Davis

TABLE OF CONTENTS

INTRODUCTION
"THE ARREST"

The police cars pulled up in front of the house and the officers came out and walked with authority to the front door with the high fence and golden door; seems like they found their man. The strobing lights from the police cars fall on the kids' faces, as they peeped through the lattice of the front door. Before their mom could tell them to get away from the door, there was an authoritative knock on the door. Even if they wanted to hide, the lights on the kids' faces told the officers someone was home.

"Get off that window kids!" their mom yelled.

She was, needless to say, more than surprised to see a police car parked in front of their house, but hearing the officers knock on the door was definitely a first for this family. She opened the door slowly and there were two police officers in plain clothes and others in blue.

"Can I help you?" asked the lady.

"Hello ma'am, is Mr. Kally home?"

"Yes, but is there a problem?"

"We have a warrant for his arrest ma'am," as they flashed their badges and a piece of paper in front of the lady.

"What's the matter, what did he do? She asked.

"Ma'am! That question is for the investigators. Just show us where he is."

She took them down to the basement, to the man cave, as the officers followed closely behind. She knocked and after some time, the door opened. The officers, seeing their chance moved quickly, cuffed him, read him his rights, and took him to the car outside. The charge… child pornography.

"Watch your head sir!" as they held his head and guided him to the back of the police car. He turned and looked at his family one last time before the car pulled away, and the sound of the slamming police car door seemed to signify the end of the grace period he had abused for so long. He heard his daughter crying and asking her mom, "Mom, where are they taking Dad?" "I don't know hon, but we'll find out soon."

CHAPTER 1
HOW IT ALL STARTS

1 Corinthians 15:33
Do not be misled: Bad company corrupts good character. (NIV)

"Good character going bad is like a beast escaping its cage; it will be hard to capture it again!" Israelmore Ayivor

1

How It All Starts

> ← →

THE GENERATIONAL CURSE

The above scenario is no longer uncommon among people that claim to be Christians, whether they are evangelicals or orthodox. More and more men's/women's infidelities are being exposed, and it seems the ladies are catching up with the men for time lost. Sexually deranged men are pressuring their wives into open relationships where each party is allowed to indulge in their individual sexual fantasy without any repercussion. This includes lawmakers, businessmen, and even the clergy. From sex toys to sex partners, strangers are appearing in the bedroom, and marriages across the world are feeling the repercussions, as the definition of sexy has evolved from cute to gross. Note that I'm not saying everyone's bed is defiled, but there's a significant amount of believers whose bed needs a *Holy Ghost cleansing*, and I believe that's why the Lord has me writing this book. I was one of those believers, but the

Lord delivered me, and after my deliverance, He commissioned me to strengthen those struggling in this area.

The other day, I posted on social media that no one is born gay/lesbian and that if they cry out to God for deliverance, He'll gladly bring them out of that bondage. It sparked a few nods of approval in the form of "likes," but I had someone that objected strongly and I was surprised, not because of the objection, but because this person is a Christian and also what was asked later by this individual. This person asked me, "How about generational curses?" I thought about it and was about to concede to that view point, but then the answer came to me in an instant string of thoughts so clear, I knew it had to be the Holy Spirit. We've all heard of testimonies of people who were delivered from different types of addictions. For many, the addiction started in the early days of their lives and then continued until it got out of control; sadly, some never recover but die in that state and end up in hell. So of course, when this question of generational curses came up, it got my attention.

My answer was simple: "God protects the young until they get to the age of accountability, and then they will have to make that choice whether or not to accept the action that will eventually lead to an addiction." It's the same concept with accepting Jesus Christ as Lord of our lives or rejecting Him. A choice has to be made. If God can't protect the children, then we can say He's not a fair judge and cannot judge righteously when someone stands before Him waiting to go to heaven or hell. Satan knows this all too well and so he fights hard to get into the minds of children, so he can enslave them for the entirety of their lives. Someone may say, "Well pastor, I've had sexual thoughts since an early age, and they never stopped, until I got into pornography." Well, allow me to tell you how I got hooked on pornography. Maybe that will clear up the confusion a little.

MY EXPERIENCE

Before I proceed, I must state that I'm sharing this and other intricate and personal parts of my life not to arouse sexual desire in anyone, but to give an account of how easy sexual addictions can start and prevail in anyone. I was raised in a loving home in Sierra Leone/West Africa. Sex was on my mind since I could remember, and being raised in a family that didn't know the Lord until I was about seven-years-old didn't help either. Sex was a taboo subject in my household and so neither my mom, nor my dad talked to me about the dangers of a sexual addiction. It was assumed that, as children, we weren't thinking of such things, but that was so far from the truth it was ridiculous. Like I said earlier, sex was on my mind all the time and even though I didn't indulge in it until I was a teen, it was like I was free falling. I knew I was headed for a crash if someone didn't break my fall. Unfortunately, this became a self-fulfilling prophecy that I would suffer from for many years to come.

On a very hot and sunny day, my stepmom sent me to get something from the room, I believe it was a pot, and it was behind the door of the bedroom. Please picture this: I grew up in a two room house with one used as the living room and the other used as the master bedroom where my father and my stepmom slept; there were seven of us in that house. Everything was tightly packed and the spot where the pot was located was where the open door (that door never closed) and the foot of the bed met, so needless to say, it was tight. I always had to squeeze myself through to get to the back of the door with my private part firmly pressed against that door. I had done this maybe hundreds of times, but on this particular day, all of a sudden, I felt my body going into a spasm and a tingly, hot sensation ran through my entire body, as semen ejaculated for the first time from me, unintentionally. Well, I was about twelve years of age, so I guess I had officially entered puberty. A lot of things happened all of a sudden, as I sat down pondering the whole experience.

First of all, I realized I just experienced the thing my school mates were bragging about doing all the time. I would later realize this is the experience that gets addicts deeper and deeper into bondage, as they chase the feeling of the "initial fix." Secondly, I was torn between a feeling of pleasure and one of guilt and lastly, I was faced with the actual choice of "do I chase the feeling of this new fantasy, or resist the urge?" Unfortunately, I chose the 3rd option and the pleasure of masturbation led to a long battle with sexual bondage, even after I rededicated my life to Jesus Christ. Was that initial action sin? I don't believe so, but the subsequent ones were definitely sinful, as I made deliberate decisions to relive that first experience. So, back to the question of the individual of generational curses; I believe that God will protect the children until they reach the age of accountability and then they'll have to make a choice. This, of course, does not take away from the fact that a child raised in a dysfunctional home stands a greater risk of being a repeat offender of what has been rehearsed before him/her. However, let's not ignore the fact that choices play a role here.

ONE MORE EXAMPLE

I was sure of the explanation of the generational curse, but it seemed God wanted me to see another example of it, so He allowed me to see an old recording on *YouTube* of Sid Roth, the investigative reporter on the supernatural, interviewing a lady by the name Francina Norman. She gave a narration of a young lady and her son that came to her meeting. The Lord showed the lady, Prophetess Francina, that the boy was struggling with a homosexual spirit and asked the mom permission to rebuke that spirit from him, but she refused. Years later, the mom came back to one of her meetings and asked this Prophetess if she remembered her, and sister Francina said, "Yes." She went on to tell the prophetess that her son is a full blown homosexual, because she refused the prayer of the woman of God. At that young age, the demon was lurking and simply sending homosexual thoughts to the mind of the boy, until he came to the age of accountability. That's when you hear people make statements like this, "I've always been attracted to same-sex individuals." What they don't know is that the enemy was feeding them with those thoughts and they thought it was theirs.

It definitely was in my case because before the encounter, I described of myself as having the opportunity of having sex with girls my age (yes, at that young teen age, some as a challenge or dare), and I refused them all. However, after my encounter, I was looking for the opportunity and because of that breakdown in my personal morals at that young age; I eventually gave into the pressure when I was a teenager. This is how any addiction starts, there has to be a willingness to indulge in the sinful action, even when there's a generational curse operating. But if that spirit is not rebuked, the child will eventually become addicted to that family curse.

<u>POWER OF YOUR WILL</u>

Before we go too far into this book, I want to point out something the Holy Spirit taught me. It will be pertinent to what we have to discuss in the future, as it relates to choices. It is not a secret that man has three parts (spirit, soul, and body). This is one of the first things a Christian is taught when he/she gives their life to the Lord. However, what we seem not to agree on is where the spirit and soul go after death. I've read much literature on this subject and some seem to state the Bible does not make a difference between spirit and soul, but classify both as the same. This may be true, but then the Holy Spirit led me to Genesis 2:7:

"And the LORD God formed man of the dust of the ground, and breathed into his nostrils the breath of life; and man became a living being."

He also showed me Ecclesiastes 12:7:

"Then the dust will return to the earth as it was, And the spirit will return to God who gave it."

In Genesis 2:7, we see that breath, or the spirit, in man comes from God and we see that breath going back to God and the body returning to the dust in Ecclesiastes 12:7.

The soul is the seat of the intellect, affections, and will and this is the part of the human that makes decisions. This is the part of me that accepted the sexual experience I just described as a pleasurable encounter, and repeated it until it became an addiction. Of course, this was compounded by the fact that I drifted away from the Lord after accepting Him as my Lord and Savior at a very young age. A person's spirit, which is the breath of God, will return to God after death, even if they were not born again. But the soul goes to either of two places, heaven or hell by the choices it makes, and the greatest of those choices is either accepting or rejecting

Jesus Christ as Lord and Savior. That's why God says, "the soul that sins will die" (Ezekiel 18:20). So, I believe there is a time in anyone's life that he/she has to choose between a life that honors God and one that dishonors Him. The power in the will of a human is so strong, not even God can change it if he/she decides to go against a God choice. God allows this to be so, because He wants us to serve Him willingly and out of love, instead of fear. This is the reason men and women are in heaven or hell today. It's called *choices*.

BUSTED

In March 2001, my wife rejoined me in Germany. We had been separated for 4 ½ years because two months after we got married, I left her in Sierra Leone, joined the US Army, spent a year in South Korea, and then got stationed in Germany; we hadn't seen each other since January 1997. During that time, I developed a porn habit that I didn't know would keep me bound for a long time. I thought I could quit anytime I wanted to, but that proved harder and more complicated than I thought. In that same year, something happened that I'm not proud of, but was very happy God allowed it to happen. Just as most families, the wife goes to bed at about 10pm, while the husband stays up watching late night T.V. or surfing the web. My wife went to bed. I got excited, because it was time for me to watch my *secret* show, so I left the T.V. on with sound, pretending I was watching it and went over to the computer. But something happened that night that does not usually happen: MY WIFE GOT UP, just to see what was taking me so long to come to bed. She met me on the computer watching "my secret show;" the look on her face broke my heart. Gentlemen, if you've ever been there you understand that look of disappointment on your love's face. Ladies, I know you feel betrayed, but please before you pack your bags and leave or throw this book away in disgust, on behalf of all men in that scenario, please read along.

There are four ways the above scenario can go:

1. You can choose to join him/her.

2. You can choose to be distant and never trust your spouse again.

3. You can choose to leave him/her and you won't be wrong, because this is adultery.

4. You can choose to forgive him/her and work with him/her, especially with the help of your pastor(s) or a counselor.

If you choose option 1, remember that you're joining him in his sin and that's like using drugs to fight a drug problem. You never get delivered and also run the risk of being addicted, as well. The problem with option 2 is that both parties will never enjoy an intimate relationship again, because of trust issues. The feelings of inadequacy can be so deep that most women can't, and will never, be at peak performance. The question is how can you compete with someone whose image has been altered for the purpose of sex? Even if you can, the desired image of lust changes so rapidly in your spouse's mind from maybe a skinny model to an oversized woman that you don't stand a chance. Option 3 is biblical, as Jesus winked at that option in Matthew 19:8 but remember, He said, "In the beginning it was not so," so even though it is biblical, there's still a better option. The truth is God hates divorce.

RISE UP

I'm so glad my wife chose option 4 and even though deliverance didn't come instantly, it came finally, but that may never have happened if she hadn't gotten out of bed to check. I'm calling on ladies especially (the Holy Spirit is), to stop ignoring the inner witness of the Holy Spirit and rise up with wisdom to confront your husband's struggling with this issue. If you have a wife struggling with this, then confront her, too. Too many spouses know of, or are at least suspicious of, the sexual misconducts of their spouses, but choose to remain silent. You know what? Your silence is killing your marriage without your knowledge. The warnings to prevent the scenario in the introduction of this book come to too many households way before the police make that dreadful knock on the door. Some of you have had dreams of it, but you're waiting for the opportune time to confront him. I know you're scared, but for his soul please confront him/her before that precious soul goes astray and eventually ends up in hell. So, rise up and gently interfere with the secret activities of the "man cave." If you're met with fierce resistance, start praying because most likely, there's an activity going on he doesn't want you know about.

What most of us don't realize is that the Lord is counting on us to confront the issue head on. He's the one tugging on your heart to do it, and He's definitely the One causing me to write this so you can be inspired to do it. He says in Ezekiel 3:18:

"When I say to a wicked person, 'You will surely die,' and you do not warn them or speak out to dissuade them from their evil ways in order to save their life, that wicked person will die for their sin, and I will hold you accountable for their blood."

I know what you're thinking… your husband or wife is not a wicked person and loves Jesus. I cannot disagree with you that he/she does love Jesus, but that's exactly the point I'm emphasizing. Continuous sin weakens your resolve to fight it off and you accept it as your fate, which eventually turns your heart away from God and makes you wicked. It almost did that to me and I loved Jesus too, so I'm telling you it's something that has to be addressed and not ignored.

CHAPTER 2

THE SANCTITY OF THE MARRIAGE BED

**Proverbs 15:15
Drink water from your own cistern,
And running water from your own well.
(NKJV)**

"The only problem with sex outside of the marriage bed is that God's perpetually absent, and that my friend is a big deal."
~ Albert Amara

2

The Sanctity of the Marriage Bed

— ⊹ ⊱ —

"Marriage is honorable in all, and the bed undefiled: but whoremongers and adulterers God will judge." (Hebrews 13:4)

Have you ever thought of why God said "the bed undefiled" and not the man or the woman in the above scripture? Is God more concerned about a mere bed than a life, or is a material thing more precious in His eyes than us? These are questions I asked myself as I meditated on this scripture, but then on October 17, 2017, the Holy Spirit gave me an epiphany on this scripture. Imagine your house as the Jewish temple, which was divided into three parts:

1. **The Outer Court**: where only the general assembly of Israelites could enter. No foreigner was even allowed, except those who had been circumcised in the flesh and in heart (Ezekiel 44:9).

2. **The Holy Place**: where only the priests enter and in there they offer blood, oil, incense, and bread to God.

3. **Holy of Holies:** where only the high priest enters and he does so only once a year.

When it comes to sexuality, let's assume the house as the whole temple itself; the rooms you allow strangers access to is the *outer court*. Most of you will understand this because you don't allow just anyone access into your home, unless they have been circumcised in the heart or rather, you've gained their trust. The bedroom is the *holy place* as access is restricted maybe only to you, your spouse, and close family members, like your kids. But, the *holy of holies* is the bed where the most private thing between you and your spouse is done, and no one should be allowed there. In Isaiah 57:7, God used the metaphor of a bed to describe how detestable idolatry was to Him, but was this just a metaphor, or was it a literal correlation of the sin of fornication/adultery to that of idol worship? I strongly believe there's a strong connection between the two, and I'll explain in the next sub-section. Of course, I'm not only talking of the physical, or else you wouldn't even allow your children on your bed, but just as you protect these physical areas of your home, God wants you to protect the marriage covenant, spiritually and physically. A man/woman cannot carry their bed physically with them, but in the spirit realm they do, and it is the duty of demons to cause you to defile it. Your duty is to honor God on that bed.

WHY THE BED SHOULD BE UNDEFILED

"On a lofty and high mountain you have set your bed; even there you went up to offer sacrifice." (Isaiah 57:7)

"Then the Babylonians came to her, to the bed of love, and in their lust they defiled her. After she had been defiled by them, she turned away from them in disgust." (Ezekiel 23:17)

There's a connection between sexual sin (especially pornography) and idolatry that cannot be ignored. Both thrive on one principle: the objectivity of an image in the mind of the one practicing it. In Ezekiel 23, when God was exposing the idolatry of Samaria and Judah, He related them to prostitutes committing sexual sins. God called Samaria, *Oholah* and Judah He called *Oholibah*. He was married to both as we see in Ezekiel 16, but they were unfaithful. In chapter 23:14-16, we see that Judah carried her sexual promiscuity even farther. She was caught up in pornography, as she lusted after the figures of men portrayed on the walls (proof of pornography, as there were only still pictures in those days). Judah objectified the men she saw on those still pictures and sent messages to them to come to her, and they came in their numbers. When they came, they went straight to her bed that was sacred and consecrated to her God and defiled it (verse 17), and she was full of disgust toward her lovers after they were done with her, because she realized it wasn't all that great. This is why demons of lust are trying to defile your bed, because they know if sin rules your life, God can't stay; not because He doesn't love you, but because He's a holy God and can't compete with sin.

God loves marriage and since He commanded the undefiled married bed whenever you and your spouse are united in sexual harmony, He's glorified and not appalled by the sight. Just as worship prepares our hearts to get into the deepest form of communication with God, likewise sex between a husband and wife prepares and ushers them into the deepest form of communication. Therefore, the place where this type of activity is done becomes sacred and set apart to the Lord. This is why a place where believers unite corporately and regularly in worship is a powerful and holy place, as it becomes a place of worship set apart unto the Lord. I've personally witnessed this in our congregation; some people get healed even without me praying, because of the mighty presence of the Lord, as prayers are offered every day in this sanctuary. Some people have even seen angels ministering to God's people here at *Agape Word Embassy*. I know you've heard of stories of the Azusa street revival where people saw the glory of God in the form of a physical fire; fire trucks were called, but they found it was not an ordinary fire. I believe these will become a common sight in the future, but what's awesome is that same type of anointing will transfer to marriage unions, because of unity.

On the other hand, we have to realize that Satan, our adversary, mimics our God, so just as God loves an undefiled bed, demons love and are attracted to a defiled bed. I'll relate that type of attraction to that between a swarm of flies to a filthy surface. A defiled bed is a *hot spot* or a *rechargeable spot* for demons, warlocks, and witches. Just as angels are drawn to a place of worship, so likewise demons are attracted to a sinful atmosphere. Imagine for a minute how people flock to coffee shops and any public business with Wi-Fi capability. For many travelers, it's the only way they can access the internet, as they're far from their home network, which normally gives them connectivity to their devices. Just like God sends His angels to a place of worship, so the enemy sends his demons to a hotspot like a bed where sexual promiscuity is taking place. This is why when sexual sin increases in city, violence abounds, because it attracts other demons. It's not just sex, but demon worship as Isaiah 57:7 states, and also a rechargeable area for demons. That's why they hate your prayers and will do anything to tempt you to defile your bed. The proliferation of godliness rids them of hotspots in any city or nation – Proverbs 14:34.

IDOLATRY AND SEX

Also in Exodus 32:6 scripture tells us:

"And they rose up early on the morrow, and offered burnt offerings, and brought peace offerings; and the people sat down to eat and to drink, and rose up to play."

This is the case where Moses had gone up to Mount Sinai to receive the Ten Commandments from the Lord and the people said he was taking too long, so they got Aaron to make them a molten calf that they said would lead them into the Promised Land. So, the people brought burnt offerings and peace offerings to the calf which was idol worship, but then why did they rise up to play? That phrase "rose up to play" is written in many forms by other Bible translations. Some of these are "pagan revelry," "make merry," and even "orgy." All of those translate to sexual sin and it showed us the strong connection between sex and idolatry. The Israelites had apparently seen this in Egypt, or in the nations in close proximity to Egypt, and wanted to practice it. As early as 1450 BC (the time of the exodus out of Egypt), the Israelites worshipped the fire god Molech of the Canaanites, Philistines, Arameans, and Semitic peoples and later, Phoenicians. One of the many ways to worship this god was to engage in anal sex, as they passed their children through the fire as a sacrifice. They would also drink the semen of their sex partners for reasons best known to them, and it was for these wicked sins God wiped out of the land and gave it to Israel.

You may be saying, "Well, that does not affect me because I don't have a sex problem nor do I worship idols." Well, let's go back to the Old Covenant and see. We see two main things that brought a separation between God and His children after He gave them the land He'd promised them. Those two things were idolatry and sexual sins. We see the parallel of that today in many cultures; most people don't have physical idols, but are so connected to things and anything that replaces God has become an idol in anyone's life. Although this is not everyone's case because sex is not a problem for some people, but I believe that as the scripture linked those two sins in Exodus 32 and all through the book of the Prophets, whenever one is present, the other is not too far behind. A good example is the fascination and eventual addiction of mobile devices among our kids (even Christian ones); it makes pornography so readily available. What's interesting is that many didn't get the device for porn, but because there was a shift in love from God to the device, it makes them so vulnerable to the attacks of porn advertisement. If left unchecked, those two will continue to increase until they eventually destroy the victim.

SEX IS A GIFT FROM GOD

Let's get one thing straight, sex is not a bad thing/word. God created it and told the first man/woman (Adam and Eve) to be fruitful, multiply, and replenish the earth. This was not an ambiguous statement; it meant having sex, not just holding hands. The only problem with that was that this couple was in God's Garden and His presence was so overwhelming and satisfying that they forgot about that command. It wasn't until their fall that they fulfilled that commandment of God (Genesis 4:1) which goes to show us that as important as sex is, there's something even more important and more satisfying, and that's God's presence. That's why there'll be no sex in heaven, because we'll be in God's presence and we'll not even have a desire for each other sexually, regardless of the fact that a man and woman were husband and wife on earth. But, let me pump your brakes and get your mind back to earth, because we're not yet in heaven, and God doesn't want you to burn with sexual passion while waiting on heaven, especially if you're married.

God wants you have fun and enjoy this pleasurable exercise He created, as long as it's with your own spouse and no one else. Any other member invited is an invasion of privacy and it comes with serious repercussions, even though many don't know this. However, don't take my word for it; let's see God's thoughts on this subject in Proverbs 5:15-17:

"Drink water from your own cistern, and running water from your own well. Should your fountains be dispersed abroad, streams of water in the streets? Let them be only your own, and not for strangers with you."

What I've noticed is that God cares about our physical pleasure as much as He does our spiritual. When it comes to sex, you don't need a handbook or video tutorial to teach you how to be good. Since He created it, He'll always be there to show you how to pleasure your spouse, so you won't need strangers in your bedroom. In the above scripture, He encourages us to drink deep from the fountain of sexual pleasure but like I already stated, it's on one condition; it should be with our own spouse. If I'm not mistaken, sex is the only thing the God of heaven, who's beyond generous, commands us not to share. I'm still searching for another thing He told us not to share; if you find it, let me know.

WHERE'S YOUR SOUL DURING INTIMACY? "SOUL TIES"

That may sound like a trick question, but it's not; it means exactly what it's asking: where are you during the most intimate time with your spouse? Are you there with him/her or are you somewhere else? By the words "somewhere else," I don't mean being bored out of your mind because this has become a chore and you just want to get it over with and get on to the next agenda of the day. I've noticed that women will do that a lot, even though it's not exclusively limited to them. A man, on the other hand, will have sex with his wife and be miles away with someone else in his imagination, especially if she's not satisfying him, or if his soul is connected to someone else or the models in porn movies. I know this because I was one of those men, but the Lord has set me free from such bondage. The late man of God, Edwin Louis Cole, called that "vaginal masturbation" in his book "Money, Sex, and Communication," but we might as well change that name because it's not unique to only men in this 21st century. So in essence, the Holy Spirit is asking who are you thinking of during sex and if the answer is not your spouse, it should bother you. Lots of people struggle with this and interestingly, they've come to accept it as harmless but of course, that's a lie from Satan and nothing can be farther from the truth. It's called a *soul tie* and is very dangerous to the health of any marriage.

Many, especially Christians, don't want the stigma of divorce, but are unwilling to fix this seemingly "small thing." Let me remind you that it's the little foxes that spoil the tender grapes (Song of Solomon 2:15), so this is not a little matter. If you fail to fix this little area in your life, you're inviting demons in your home and while you may not be affected because you're the doorway, your family might. Just like in a parasitic relationship, the host will stay alive long enough for the pathogens to be transmitted by the parasite, but eventually the host, too, will die. The adversary comes to steal, kill, and destroy and in a family setting, he is the parasite while the person with the lust problem is the host, so please don't be a host for Satan's woes. One thing Satan knows is God's Word and he knows the curse goes to the 4th generation, so he tries to keep that door open to affect your family. I know you've heard of hereditary illnesses like cancer and heart disease; these are the result of the curse, but no matter what generation of the curse you're in, you can break it in the name of Jesus Christ. Legally, the curse stops at the 4th generation, but the blessing goes to a thousand generations and if you're in Christ, the blessing is your only entitlement. Refuse the curse!

BREAKING SEXUAL SOUL TIES!!!

Sexual *soul ties* are very real and can be formed between two people when they have consensual sexual intercourse with each other for the first time. The experience can be so pleasurable that a bond is formed. This bond is so strong that whenever any of those in it have sexual intercourse with a person they don't share that connection with, they won't enjoy it, because they'll be imagining the person they have the soul tie with, even if they've been physically separated. That's why virgins fall in love and are connected to the man they willingly allow to break their hymen, until the connection is broken in the spirit. God knows a *soul tie* will be established, that's why He wants us to wait until marriage and not be connected with the wrong person in our matrimonial beds.

Ephesians 5:31 tells us, *"For this cause shall a man leave his father and mother, and shall be joined unto his wife, and they two shall be one flesh."*

This also explains 1 Corinthians 6:16 which says, *"What? Know ye not that he which is joined to an harlot is one body? For two, saith he, shall be one flesh."*

It is also important and worth mentioning that *soul ties* can be established with the models on porn videos. This is rather dangerous, because the image in the person's mind changes and no woman can compete with that demon of lust. There has to be a breaking away from that soul tie.

To break a sexual soul tie, you have to repent of the sexual sin committed and if any gift was given, it's very appropriate to get rid of it no matter how expensive the gift was, or else the physical presence of such a gift will keep the soul tie in place. Next, you have to renounce the soul tie verbally. That is done by speaking out loud that you are no longer a part of it and then in the name of Jesus, break its holding power over your life. You may have to do this over and over, because Satan never wants to let his captives go free. For many people, this is the confusing part because they'll start having nightmares and sexual dreams, even after renouncing the soul tie. This is where persistence pays off; the devil may be pesky, but you have the ability to outlast him, because you have the spirit of perseverance in you. Continue renouncing it verbally even after the first try; the Holy One of Israel will come to your aid, but He wants to see if you're serious about your deliverance. I want to emphasize here that you have to consciously disengage from images of other sex partners in an intimate moment with your spouse and train your soul to do that. It may not sound pleasurable at the moment, but ask the Holy Spirit to train your soul; the pleasure will follow after. It's more important to please God than yourself.

BEWARE OF SATAN'S DEEP SECRETS

When I was reading up on material for this book, I came across a video of a lady whose boyfriend was bored beyond comprehension when making love to her. One night, she caught him watching porn and noticed the delight on his face, as the porn actress said trigger words that got him off. She was appalled, but kept it a secret and decided she'll use this to her advantage and later went back to find what triggered men sexually and why many love porn so much. So, she watched a whole bunch of porno videos herself and interviewed many interesting people. She came up with a manual for the everyday woman that worked from teenagers to ladies in their 80s. By this time, I was intrigued and decided to use the material in this book, but something happened. At night when I sat to write, I had a very strong sexual desire like I used to have when I was younger, the type that used to drive me to watch porn and masturbate. I knew I was under attack, so I GOT UP TO FIGHT. I started meditating on scriptures on sexual purity until the feeling lifted. Then, the Holy Spirit spoke to me, not audibly, but in the way He normally speaks to me. He impressed in my spirit that there are many ways to achieve sexual pleasure, but not all are His. Oh how He waits to teach us. Then, He reminded of a scripture in Revelations 2:24 of Satan's deep secrets.

I was amazed, repented for watching the seemingly innocent video, and decided against using any of that material. Just as I watched that video innocently, a lot of believers are, as well. They're using Satan's *deep secrets* and sleeping with the devil without even realizing it, and in the process, defiling their marriage beds. God wants to restore your sexual appetite for your spouse and make both of you enjoy your intimate time together, but you have to start by asking Him to help you. Don't be surprised if you start getting attacks in your dreams when you start getting serious to have an undefiled bed. I used to wonder why I didn't have dreams of snakes, until I got serious to rid my life of sexual demons. The reason is already explained above but this is true, "Whenever demons see their dominion over your family is threatened, they'll fight harder to stay in that family, but fight the good fight of faith and kick them out." They don't need a prolonged notice to move out, but an immediate eviction order; they will kick and scream through your emotions for reasons to stay. Please don't flinch in your decision; kick them out!!!

CHAPTER 3

STRANGERS IN THE BEDROOM

Proverbs 15:17
Let them be only your own,
And not for strangers with you. (NKJV)

"These two words are diametrically opposed to each other, yet every day we hear the atrocities and the horror stories of "strangers" in the "bedroom." ~Albert Amara

3

Strangers in the Bedroom

→ ←

STRANGERS ARE FORBIDDEN

Today, more and more couples are looking for ways to resurrect their sexual appetites or increase the pleasure, and in the process are inviting strangers in the form of sexual partners and paraphernalia into their bedrooms. Their intensions are good, but the problem is that God's original intent for the sexual experience was for it to be solo and not shared by the masses. Let's look at the scripture we looked at in chapter 2: Hebrews 13:4. In the original King James it states:

"Marriage is honorable in all, and the bed undefiled: but whoremongers and adulterers God will judge."

Since the King James translation was the only one available for a long time for English speakers before other translations started emerging, many people had a wrong understanding of that scripture. Many that didn't study out the scripture thought it meant anything goes in the bedroom, as long as it's approved by either party in the relationship. But that's not what the Holy Spirit was saying through the Apostle. When you look at the Latin translation, the word that translates "bed" is *koite* and it is in the nominative form.

Basically, what that means (so we don't get tangled in the grammar of the language) is that the sentence should have read "the marriage bed is to be undefiled." This seems not to be a problem today, as more and more people are getting exposed to newer translations and understand the meaning of that scripture. However, for those who want to be corrupt, they will continue to use that as an excuse and get more and more entangled in the web of sexual bondage. Speaking of a web, there's one thing peculiar about a spider's web that's worth mentioning here and that is when prey gets entangled in there, it will take another source to free it from there. Most prey don't even know it's a trap, until they're too far gone in it and when they want out, the web maker strikes. In the area of sex, many inviting these strangers into their bedrooms don't even know it's risky, until it's too late. One thing is for sure, these sexual fantasies are not innocent.

I'm reminded of a fellow US soldier almost two decades ago (in 1999). We met at our AIT (Advanced Individual Training) after basic training at Ft. Gordon, Georgia, and he told me and some other soldiers a story that still brings me a level of sadness for this soldier whenever I think of it. He told us he and his wife agreed to have a threesome with another woman. Since it was so good (according to him), the wife asked if they can do it again but this time, with another guy. They did and it led to the breakdown of the marriage, because the other man pleased this soldier's wife too well, and she left her husband for the new guy, while the husband was in military training. These are the repercussions of sin, regardless of what name tag we put on that sin. And for those that say this type of lifestyle is harmless; they have not experienced it firsthand because if had, they will not be saying that. Unfortunately, I didn't stay in contact with this soldier, so I don't know if he got his wife back, but needless to say, these situations never end well and some end in a tragedy. This goes to show that nothing good comes out of sin, even if it looks harmless. Most venomous snakes look so cute and harmless, but when you try playing with it, you'll find they're very harmful.

WHY IS GOD TAKING THE FUN AWAY SOMEONE ASKS?

God loves us and His laws are not there to enslave us, but to give us more enjoyment. I'm talking of the God that says there's joy in His presence and eternal pleasures at His right hand. However, for Him to give us that, He has to keep us within the parameters of righteousness, because that's the only place of true safety. This is the only place God can legally protect His children; any other place will be out of His NAO (normal area of operation) although sometimes, He'll reach down and scoop one of His creation from the abyss of sin. He's God; He can do that any time He feels like, because of His great mercy. God's not trying to take the fun away and let us live boring lives but in His wisdom, He gives us these boundaries, so we can be protected from the effects of sin. Take sexual diseases like AIDS or syphilis for example; people mostly acquire them through promiscuity. The world says, "Enjoy your life with multiple sexual partners and maybe you'll find the right one for you." God, in His wisdom, says to us, "Stay sexually pure, so you don't die prematurely before you find *the one*." A wise man/woman will listen and stay clear of these pitfalls, because even if he/she doesn't die of one of these diseases, the cost of chasing love through sexual experimentation can be too much. God's wisdom is infinite. If you stick with Him, you won't have to go through so many sexual partners to get to "the one," Mr. or Mrs. Right.

Sexual sin, like any other sin, is progressive and if left unchecked, will upgrade itself to full scale lawlessness, as we saw happen in many places in the Bible. It was what happened when Moses went up to Mount Sinai to receive the Ten Commandments in Exodus 32: 6; the scripture says the people got up to "play." That was not an ordinary play, but one that involved wild partying, which most of the time is accompanied with drinking and sexual orgies. Also when Sodom and Gomorrah were about to be destroyed in Genesis 19, God sent two angels to Sodom and Lot took them into his home, not wanting them to sleep outside. The men of the city, however, had other plans; they came over to Lot's house and demanded to have sex with the angels. This showed that the city had no moral boundaries and sinful pleasure was the continual meditation of the people so for that, God destroyed them. Fast forward to today: that account means if we were living in those days, none of our relatives would be safe from such perversion. If the men of the city wanted to have sex with your fourteen-year-old virgin daughter, as long as you don't have the means to stop them, they will have her. These are the effects of a lawless society, and that's why we have to stay within God's boundaries.

GOD'S THE AUTHORITY, NOT MAN

Consent by both parties to have multiple partners in the bedroom doesn't make it right; it makes it consensually wrong. We don't have the legal or spiritual authority to overrule God's laws just because we consent to break them. Marriage and sex in the marriage is His idea and as such, He gets to create the law that governs it, not us. He said in Genesis 2:24

"Therefore a man shall leave his father and mother and be joined to his wife, and they shall become one flesh."

Do you notice He said the two shall become one flesh? That means the man and the woman shall become one flesh, not multiple people shall become one flesh. An open, or polyandrous, marriage is not love but instead, lust in its truest sense. It cannot be sacred if what's supposed to be intimate is shared with more than two people. This goes to show us that nothing in man is good; every intention of the thoughts of his heart is continually evil (Genesis 6:5). Without abiding in God's laws, we will continue to devise ways to commit sin and eventually destroy our generation, because sin leads to death. We don't have any good in us without Jesus Christ, because our flesh naturally wants to return to dust (or filth) from where it came from (Genesis 3:19).

Look at what we've achieved when we took it upon ourselves to be the authority for marriage. We've had male and female same-sex partners, bestiality, and now the concept of ageless love that many *so called* advanced nations are flirting with.

"Well, all of these are not new and have been with man since the dawn of the ages," someone will point out. That's exactly why God has to be the authority for marriage in any nation if that nation wants to continue being a nation. The moment we feel we've become too sophisticated for God and substitute His laws for ours, we start dying as a nation and give permission to demonic forces to invade our land. The Israelites are a perfect example for any nation today that seeks to part from the God of heaven. In the Bible, anytime they departed from the ways of their God, their enemies overpowered them and had them as slaves and most of the time; God allowed that to happen after repeated warnings. Interestingly, anytime they chose to abandon God, they became viler that the nations they copied from and sexual promiscuity was right in the middle of their disobedience. Therefore, judgment was always harsh on them. Now, let's look at some of the strangers in the bedroom.

WATCHING PORN TOGETHER

During my time in the military, I heard of a lot of kinky stuff people did to spice up their sex lives, and one of those was watching porn together. Some men even enjoyed the sick fetish of other men having sex with their wives; Satan is evil deceiving a man to give up his sovereignty (if you may) in a marriage relationship for a sexual fantasy. Most people don't understand why Christians see porn as something bad if both parties approve of it. Simply put, it is inviting a stranger into your bedroom, and this is a stranger that is as lethal as a rattlesnake. It may seem very exciting or appealing and may promise you no harm, but just like a venomous snake, have nothing to do with this relationship destroyer. When you least expect, it'll strike and leave its venom deep within the immune system of your relationship that you'll need divine intervention to recover. I know you've heard of *success stories* of those who porn supposedly helped. Let me let you in on a secret, "even the devil has success stories to deceive the gullible." Most of those people are not truly saved and if they are, for the most part, they are compromising to put their sexual needs above the Word of God. If Jesus says we should not look at a woman lustfully, what makes us think looking at a naked man/woman on a screen is okay?

Too many marriages have been ruined because of this unsuspecting evil stranger, couples have allowed into their bedrooms, and as you would a good pet, they allowed it straight into their beds. Unnoticed while they slept, it came in between once loving couples and turned them into monsters, and now they rehearse what has been regurgitated to them by that demon. They don't even make love now, they just have sex and it's not only unaffectionate, but physically and emotionally painful. This is the effect of watching porn, even if it's together with your spouse, because the spirit behind porn seeks to objectify or degrade the partner being used, in order to achieve pleasure, and the partner being used will eventually resent that action or accept it. Ladies, you don't have to accept it because it may be pleasurable now, but be careful what you allow someone to call you. Remember, God changed Abram's name to Abraham for the manifestation of his destiny, so there's power in a name. Gents, why would you call "your good thing" filthy names used on porn movies, such as "slut" and much worse ones in the name of getting to a new orgasmic climax? It is demonic and comes from only one place – hell. One this is certain; lust can never be satisfied, so I'm asking you to please stop this lest it lead you to opening your marriage bed to sexual orgies (many Christians have gone this route) and eventually, hell.

PORN IS NOT IN THE BIBLE?

Some will say, "Show me where it says in the Bible, you should not watch pornography?" Really, really?" is my answer. I'll show you one scripture and leave the rest to your discretion, and that's 1 Corinthians 7:1-2. In this scripture, Paul was telling the people of Corinth that it's good for a man not to marry (this is for those who are called to that, so they can focus on the Lord's work). However, because of "sexual immoralities," or fornication, which was prevalent in the Greek/Roman culture, he cautioned each man/woman to have sex with his/her own spouse. You say what does that have to do with pornography? Please follow me: The word for fornication, or sexual immorality, in the Greek is *porneia* from where we get the word pornography and it included any type of illicit sexual activity from homosexual acts to incest and even sex with animals, so pornography is listed in God's Word many times. It's no secret that pornography in drawings and still pictures existed long before the making of the first erotic motion picture by Eugène Pirou and Albert Kirchner in 1896, and its goal was then, and is today, to arouse you sexually, not art, as is wrongly portrayed. A naked picture in your bedroom is not art. I won't even call it soft porn; it's porn, and there's nothing soft about a porn addiction.

Ancient history itself tells us that pornography has been in existence for a long time. As an example, in 1819 King Francis 1 of Naples visited the Pompeii exhibition at the Naples National

Archaeological Museum and a lot of the erotic art from the old city of Pompeii was discovered, and it brought to light the active sexual lifestyle of the Romans. It was so graphic that they were sealed from the general public and open only to upper class scholars. Also, in Ancient Egypt, there was a belief that the ebb and flow of the Nile was caused by the god of creation's ejaculation, *Min*, who is always shown with an erected penis he holds in his left hand, which is a sign of masturbation. This idea caused the Pharaohs to habitually masturbate into the Nile in a bid to ensure enough water for crops in the land. During the festival of this false god, men will masturbate openly in public.

These are not biblical, but historic proof to show that this lifestyle didn't start today, but had been in existence for ages. So, when Paul talked of sexual immoralities, or *porneia*, he was speaking of a practice that was embedded in the culture of the people of Corinth. We all know how the Greeks and Romans perfected this sinful stench. There's a connection between what the eyes see and what the hands do; that's why Jesus talked about getting rid of those two body parts in Mathew 5:29, 30 if they cause you to sin. Of course, I don't believe Jesus means to literally cut off your body parts, but to get rid of that thing that has gotten you so hooked that heaven is no longer important to you.

SEX TOYS 1

"Finally, brothers and sisters, whatever is true, whatever is noble, whatever is right, whatever is pure, whatever is lovely, whatever is admirable--if anything is excellent or praiseworthy--think about such things." (NIV)

From this passage, we see that God wants us to think about what's true, noble, right, pure, lovely, admirable, excellent, and praiseworthy. My first question about sex toys when you use it, does it make you feel or think about the above adjectives in Philippians 4:8? If not, this should be the first indication that what you're doing is wrong. Oh yeah I said it, "Wrong!" One of the things society has shifted from is calling right, right and wrong, wrong. Not everything is relative, and one of those things is *truth*. This stance for holiness in calling sin, sin should start in the church. Yes, we will be hated for it, but we have to stand and call sin for what it is and not be afraid of the repercussions. Not everything goes when it comes to God, so if when using a sex toy you start fantasizing about the size of another person's genitals because your spouse's doesn't measure up, let me say to you that you're not thinking pure thoughts and should stop using that toy. If you continue in this path, I believe you've given approval to an invisible stranger in your bedroom that now has legal access to your home. Brother/Sister, this is how demons of sexual perversion latch themselves to a family and refuses to leave. A portal was opened for them.

SEX TOYS 2 (THE THREE SIDES OF SEX)

I had known for a long time that sex was three dimensional, but reading Sheila Gregoire's blog "Wifey Wednesday: Can Christians Use Sex Toys?" gave me further proof, because she confirmed what the Holy Spirit taught me on this subject. Have you noticed that whenever you have resentment toward your spouse, the sex is not as great as when both of you are at peace? This is because there's a disconnection between both of you in the area of spirit and soul and until that is reconciled; there'll not be total satisfaction. This is one of the reasons some spouses become unfaithful, because they don't feel a connection anymore and instead of using God's Word to fix the problem, they go out of their marriage to find the missing connection with other partners. Let me ask a rather silly question. Why don't you want to bring a prostitute home and make her your wife (for those that have gone that route)? I know there are exceptions to this; some men have done that. The reason is simple: there's a disconnect in the spirit and soul realm between you and this person, even if the sex was very good and you cannot bring yourself to take the risk. This brings me to my next point.

Sex toys don't have the ability to connect people spiritually and a dependence on them can lead to masturbation when your spouse is not present, even if you think you're thinking of him/her. All it does for a married couple is connect them physically and this is dangerous, because sex is the greatest expression of erotic love. It's not just physical because when a man and woman continuously and consensually have sex, their spirit, soul, and body become united after a while. This is why after being married for a while, both start looking alike. That's why it's important to be married, because you can have great sex and be connected with each other in the soul, but true spiritual connection comes from the Father that initiated sex – Yahweh. He said it in Genesis 2:26:

"Therefore a man shall leave his father and mother and be joined to his wife, and they shall become one flesh."

I believe it's important that there be a skin to skin interaction between you and your spouse during intimacy, because during sex, many incompatibilities are fixed in the spirit and soul. I'm a witness to this, as many things I didn't use to like about my wife are now a thing of the past. On a side note, that's why we should engage in this activity regularly and not keep our partners begging for intimacy.

SEX TOYS 3 (THE ULTIMATE FANTASY)

When I was a Sergeant in the US Army, on our down time in Iraq and Afghanistan, my soldiers and others would always have casual conversations on sex and many would go into details narrating their sexual exploits (a brewing pot for masturbation and sexual perversions). At the start, I scolded them for those types of talks, but when they started avoiding me, I started compromising and soon, I was in the center of those discussions; how true Psalm 1:1-3 proved to be. On one of those conversations, a guy narrated how he can't ejaculate in a woman's vagina; he always has to pull out as in the porno movies. I thought to myself "how weird," but now I understand fully that it's not only weird, but also selfish. Now, let's apply that to sex toys and we see the same underlying selfish culture of parallel sexual and not mutual, experiences. "What do you mean pastor," you ask. Well, since many sex toys are masturbatory in nature, a dependence on them will eventually have you making love to them, instead of your spouse, and this is very selfish. Sex is designed by God to be a mutual and not a parallel experience between a husband and wife. That is why I used the example of the soldier that always had to be pull out before he climaxed to show the selfishness of it. One thing I guarantee is that unless he changes, he'll have a difficult time impregnating his wife.

The other danger in the use of sex toys is the fact that they can be totally fictional and as such, develop a fantasy that is fueled by a lie and can only be satisfied by assimilating that lie as the truth. Let's face it, most of us men are not as big as most fake penises they sell in sex shops, and we don't vibrate like those vibrators either; well, at least not me the last time I checked. Apart from the fact that I don't and will never subscribe to the peripherals of the adult industry sold in these sex shops, I will hate making my wife dependent on something that's not the real thing. Some women love being with a particular race/color of men, and so they discreetly select the color they prefer in these shops. Some may say it's harmless, but I'll say there has to be something fundamentally wrong with fantasizing about another when you have the real deal in front of you. Whatever happened to do it yourself, or are we being lazy? I know we live in the 21st century when experimentation is the rule of the day, but I keep on asking myself, "Did Abraham need those for Sarah?" Think of all the things you can do without a battery operated device and allow the Holy Spirit to bring the creativity out of you. I know it requires getting used to and "work," but the Holy Spirit is available to help.

SHOULD I BAN THE TOYS PERIOD?

So, someone will ask, "Should we stop using sex toys?" My answer to that is an emphatic, "YES!"

Have you ever wondered why an increased number of women are getting addicted to pornography and other sexual bondages today? More and more women are cheating on their husbands, as their hubbies don't seem to satisfy them sexually, and most ladies (in tears) don't even know why. They want to be faithful, but a force greater than them seems to be pulling them to that default mode. The simple answer many will give is because of the fallen nature of man, but women (even non-Christians) never used to be this open about sexual experimentation maybe since Greek/Roman days. Something happened along the line that has caused women to be so bold and open about sex, without any shame or remorse, even when caught on the wrong side of the taboos of a society. They call it liberating, but please let's recall that in the beginning, it wasn't so. In Genesis 2 after God brought Eve to Adam, it was Adam that made the move or plucked that flower called Eve, not the other way around. Eve's voice was not even heard until Genesis 3 when the devil tempted her, which Adam should have stopped.

Eve didn't need to say a word because she was well taken care of by her God and her man, Adam, until a stranger (the devil) showed up. Fast forward to today and you see the same problem with that stranger of *sex toys* in the bedroom. God told us not to make any graven images in Exodus 20:4 and that dildo, or whatever toy, can be a graven image; some ladies love their sex toys to the point of adoration, so it becomes an idol. Whether you love them to that level or not, these things are not innocent and they come with the spirits of lust on them. As a *YouTuber* puts it, these sex toys are "MANufactured," meaning they come from the minds of men who are not sanctified to our God. Man without Christ is selfish, so the sole purpose of creating these toys is to seduce and bring self-pleasure, which as we stated earlier in this chapter, is not the original intention of God creating sex. If sex is done selfishly, you can't get enough of it because you cannot quench a desire fueled by a demon, and that's the reason many can't break free from sexual sins. Start by burning all of them and don't worry about the cost or how loud your body screams for the loss. It's worth it.

CHAPTER 4
THE SPIRIT OF POTIPHAR'S WIFE

Genesis 39:7
And it came to pass after these things that his master's wife cast longing eyes on Joseph, and she said, "Lie with me."
(NKJV)

"Preventing sexual sins especially with a married woman, needs to be done two ways: proactively and actively." ~Unknown

4

The Spirit of Potiphar's Wife

> ✦ ✦

WHO'S SHE?

In Genesis 39, there's a very unique and interesting story about a young man named Joseph who was sold into slavery in Egypt and bought by a man named Potiphar, an officer of Pharaoh and captain of his guard. Without question, Potiphar was a very influential man and had a wife who had a lust problem. Personally, I believe this woman was beautiful and sophisticated, if you may, because she was (1) an Egyptian and Egyptian woman of that era loved beauty and knew the art of seduction and (2) she was the wife of a high official, so of course, she'll want to uphold that social status. It seemed to suggest that either her man was too busy with the affairs of Pharaoh and had no time for her, or she simply had a lust problem; the Bible doesn't specify. One thing was sure, she had a thing for Joseph and she was going to do everything in her power to get him to sleep with her, or she would bring him down. Today, many Christians relate every sexual deviation to the Jezebel or Delilah spirit, but know nothing about the spirit of Potiphar's wife.

This spirit is a seductive spirit and comes for one purpose and that is to stop the advancement of God's work through sex. It operates primarily from a position of higher influence/privilege to one of less influence/privilege so as much as it is about sex, power and influence is also involved. Note that the woman under this spirit's grip becomes the hunter instead of the hunted and in this case, her sex drive is stronger than a man's. In Joseph's issue in Genesis 39, Satan saw that a position of power and influence had been given to a child of God, and as you know anytime we are in charge, we rule righteously; stopping all injustice and things flow as originally designed. Our God's favor on us makes us shine more than the one that doesn't know our God. The reason Satan was afraid was that he saw redemption for God's people in a teenager called Joseph and he activated his angel of darkness who was already residing in Potiphar's wife to seduce Joseph. He wanted to stop the destiny of Joseph and as such, stop an entire nation, but God had prepared Joseph for this temptation. Please hear me on this: not that the rest of the Bible is not important, but Genesis is a book of beginnings, or "firsts," and according to Genesis 39, God gives us a pattern of how this spirit operates.

Please let's all pay attention, watch, and pray as Jesus cautioned us all so we don't fall to this spirit's deceptive schemes and traps. I believe the reason the Holy Ghost gave me this chapter on the spirit of Potiphar's wife is to expose the tactics of this spirit. You may have gotten rid of the strangers in your bedroom and think you're safe but remember, this world belongs to Satan; he's the god of it (2 Corinthians 4:4) so he has agents everywhere and can activate them at any time. So, don't be surprised when you start drawing closer to the Lord and He starts opening doors for you how temptations with the opposite sex multiply. If you're a man, you should know a spirit of Potiphar's wife has been released against you, and its goal is to defile your bed. Your obligation is to stand up to it, resist it, and expose it. It's not that women are exempt from this, but I know Satan believes in division of labor and just as almighty God has specific angels for specific tasks, that snake has demons he's assigned to carry out specific parts of his diabolical plans. For this part of the book, I'm dealing with the spirit of Potiphar's wife. Let me encourage you that God believes in you and He's counting on you to walk in the victory He's given you to defeat that enemy. Now. let's see how that spirit attacks:

1. **THE TEMPTATION**

My first pastor in Germany, Dr. Charles A. Johnson, who now pastors Victory Community Church in Arizona used to say, "You'll know how well a man treats his wife by the look in her eyes." Basically, the eye reveals a lot about how lonely, or satisfied, a woman is; same concept applies to a man. I remembered this statement and paid close attention to what the Holy Spirit was telling me about this woman's eyes in Genesis 39:7. As I stated earlier, I don't know whether or not this woman was neglected by her hubby, but one thing is sure: a woman with a "longing eye" has a lust problem. In the human body (not the soul), the area of approval or rejection of this spirit of Potiphar's wife is the eyes. It's true you may have seen her dress seductively, which may have been your first encounter with that spirit and your soul may be processing the information for approval. However, if that spirit is sent after you, it will eventually make eye contact for an approval. This spirit through Potiphar's wife cast longing or lustful eyes on Joseph making sure there was enough eye contact, but the man of God refused its advances.

Joseph was a very attractive and handsome man, as the Bible states, and the devil used that to attract Potiphar's wife to him, but I don't believe it's restricted to only handsome/attractive men. That devil is sneaky and can allow women to see something in a man others have not seen, as long as it can defile your bed; that thing is the anointing of God. Therefore, be very careful when older or influential women start giving you compliments based on your physique or appearance. It may be subtle or may sound innocent, but don't dismiss it as nothing. The Holy Spirit may be gently telling you to watch out, so if you're not bold enough to stand up to it (which I highly recommend), start speaking against it in the secret place of prayer. Personally, I had to do that with higher members of the echelon in my chain of command when I was in the US Army. Most men will give up at this stage, but you're not like "most men," you're a son of God. They see it as a great opportunity when a woman, especially one of a higher social status, is attracted to them sexually. Remember man of God, it's a trap; overcome it because phase 2 is coming.

2. THE VERBAL SEXUAL ADVANCE

So, you've refused her seductive looks and you think it's over? No my friend, it's just the beginning, this spirit is persistent. The reason you know it was sent after you is that most women will shy away after a man has rejected their sexual innuendos and undertones, but not those under the influence of this spirit. We all know how most women shy away from the topic of sex but not this spirit. It will move on to stage 2 and that's verbally telling you that it desires you sexually, whether you're married or not, and is not ashamed of it either. Potiphar's wife made this advance, but Joseph resisted that too, and told her the gospel truth, "…How then can I do this great wickedness, and sin against God?" Joseph realized two things here (1) It's a great wickedness and (2) It's against God. He realized that God was the One that promoted him to that position and sinning against Him was a great wickedness. Oh how significantly we can cut down sexual sin among God's children if we realize the importance of these two points.

No man in his right state of mind will allow another man to sleep with his wife. I know there are exceptions and some men that have that type of fetish get sexually aroused to see their wife have sex with another man, but that is a demon spirit at work. It's not natural and Joseph knew that, and told Potiphar's wife, but a woman operating under the influence of this spirit does not care about the feelings of her spouse or her marriage vow. She's selfish and all she wants is her sexual need fulfilled. Women in that state flirt with the idea of being caught to the point that the line between reality and fantasy becomes blurred by the lies they keep telling themselves. It's dangerous to play the game they're playing, because for them the riskier it is, the more sexual pleasure they get from the experience, until a tragedy, or the like, snaps them back into reality. If you're wondering how some ladies who aren't prostitutes or aren't being forced into having sex can drop their morals so low and have sex in public places, look no further; these are those ladies. They're under the influence of that demon of Potiphar's wife.

3. THE COMPROMISE

"And so it was that she spoke to Joseph [persistently] day after day, but he did not listen to her [plea] to lie beside her or be with her" (Amplified Bible).

Most people read this passage in Genesis 39:10 so fast that they fail to see the revelation there. Potiphar's wife wanted to strike a compromise with Joseph and that compromise was very subtle: to be around her or maybe lie by her, according to the translation you are reading from. It may be as simple as just lie by her side, which shows something about her. Potiphar's wife was a very lonely woman who wanted attention from a male figure and wanted it by any means necessary; she always desires that male presence around or within her vicinity. "Lying by her" is a compromise and the desired goal is that of having the person always in your thoughts. It may come by means of a nude picture on an electronic device (sexting), or being around this individual until a sexual affection is developed. Whatever it is, the final goal is to get you in bed with her, so you can defile your marriage bed. She's not worried about defiling her bed, because it's already defiled. Her goal is you and don't forget she's under the influence of a spirit and can do things that will surprise you; she's not herself.

The irony of this story here is that Joseph had no marriage bed to defile, since he was unmarried at the time of the temptation, so it may seem it didn't' apply to him. However, he realized he had to be married someday and feared his God to do anything that foolish. Joseph exemplified what a single, godly man is supposed to be like. Many are faithful to their wives, but not to God; they fail to see the eternal rewards of chastity while single and so break their sexual vows. Please let me remind everyone that there are rewards and consequences for our disobedience. Many of us did sin sexually before marriage, while being saved and are doing well today, so it may seem it doesn't matter, as grace covers all sins. However, may we never fail to realize that sin is a momentum stopper and while many of us recover and do well later on in life, some never do and unfortunately, fall deeper and deeper into that sinkhole of sin? I don't know what would have happened had Joseph yielded to the temptations of Potiphar's wife (personally I believe he would never have had the opportunity to be the 2nd in command of Egypt). One thing is certain and that is he would never have been an effective leader, and Samson was a good example of that.

THE PHYSICAL ADVANCE

Joseph had done his due diligence and kept out of the way of this woman. He knew that spirit in her wanted to get him in its office space, which is privacy, so it could ruin his reputation openly. This is where many men fail the test; they keep the temptation a secret and when we fail to expose that devil, he gets bolder. Now, I'm not saying Joseph was wrong for not exposing her because it seemed he was in a "catch 22" situation. If he had exposed her, no one would believe him, because she was the wife of Potiphar and they'll believe her over a slave. On the other hand, if he had gone ahead and slept with her, he would displease his God and lose the favor on his life. It seemed Joseph had a lot of respect for her, but she didn't care about that, she just wanted her sexual needs met. If he didn't respond to her repeated sexual advances, she was going to go to the final strike and that was to force him. This is the final move of that demon spirit in the area of temptation, because the next is rejection and exposure. So, she planned her move, waited when no one was around, and grabbed Joseph to force him into bed with her, which is the first documented proof of female attempted rape. There's nothing new under the sun; it's all in God's Word.

If there was any doubt Joseph feared God it was definitely cleared in Genesis 39:12. The spirit of Potiphar's wife attacked and Joseph ran away, leaving his clothes with her. He could have said, "Well, God will understand because He's seen that I've resisted the temptation this long and now I have no other option but to compromise and give this woman what she wants." He not only rejected her, but ran out of the house because he knew if he had stayed, he may have been overcome by the spirit in that woman through lust. Many men today think they are wiser than God in staying in the compromising situation thinking they have the power to resist it. Scripture in 1 Corinthians 6:18 commands us to "flee" which in today's English means *run* from sexual immorality. If you're in that situation, please do what Joseph did and run for your dear sanctified life, or you'll fall sooner than you think. Staying there is telling God you're wiser than Him, because He's commanded you already to run. Running away from that situation is not a sign of weakness either (as someone told me before), but a sign of strength and dominion over sexual sins.

God longs to have us in the secret place, so He can protect our privacy with His presence. His presence is what covers our nakedness, just like Adam and Eve in the Garden were not physically covered, but were not ashamed. Likewise, the master counterfeiter

Satan, who always copies our God, will try to get you in the secret place, so he can expose your nakedness. Do you see the trend here? Potiphar's wife waited for Joseph to get into a private place to strip him of his clothes, so she could get to the man's most private part of his body to rid him off the anointing on his life. Someone may say, "Well, no one would have known," but that's not true. If he had consented, it would not have stayed a secret because that devil's final goal was to expose the sin, because he knew what was at stake. The thing at stake was the salvation of an entire nation, and Joseph was the link between the promise and the fulfillment. Satan is the accuser of the brethren (Revelation 12:10) and anytime we sin, he accuses us before the Father. If Joseph had fallen to that sin that snake would have accused him in heaven, and it may have taken the children of Israel a longer time to be delivered from the famine in Israel. However, we know God's wisdom is unsearchable, so He would have used another way to bring about the promise He made to Abraham to pass (Genesis 17:4-8).

SHE GOES PUBLIC

After that demon fails to get you in bed with the physical advance, it'll want to go public to ruin your reputation, or put you in jail like it did Joseph. That's because it's been humiliated and now it wants revenge. It has presented the best carnal medium available to entice you into sin and instead of you taking advantage of the presumed privileged position, you still find courage to resist, even if you had to leave your clothes and run away. Now, that spirit is going all out to bring you down and it's got false evidence, but don't be scared; it's all *fake news*. Your God had His angels document every scenario and they're stored in heaven's roll. Sometimes, just like Joseph, the way to the palace is through a prison, because there's a butler, baker, and other prisoners you have to minister to first. Don't throw in the towel!!! What's amazing is that Joseph was never bitter, even though he was innocent. If you're innocent (and even if you're not, but have repented), stay joyful and in the spirit. While your case is being settled in heaven's court, you have ministry in that, your designated wilderness. Remain faithful there because you want to look back and be joyful of God's work done through you while in that wilderness.

Be careful when that devil goes public with your secret; it's never a good thing. Remember, he comes to steal, kill, and destroy, so there's not a single human he loves. He's incapable of love because true love only comes from the Father; therefore, any gift he gives you now is not free. He's coming back to collect his bill and trust me it's with interest. Whenever Satan goes public with your secret, the goal is to expose you so he can ruin your reputation, which is your good name and we all know the importance of a good name. There are people that have sold the rights to their name for millions; one very popular example was Muhammad Ali who sold the rights to his name for $50M in 2006. Yours is worth more than perishable money, because its true value is redeemable in the currency exchanges of heaven, but it starts right here on earth. That's why I'm so happy Joseph's story went the way it did, and not like Samson's, because it's an example to show the faithfulness of God for those that choose God's way. Samson's story is another reason to trust God's Word as the truth, because God didn't include only good guys like Joseph, but also Samson who messed up big time.

CHAPTER 5
THE SPIRITOF DAVID'S ADULTERY

Proverbs 6:32
But a man who commits adultery has no
sense; whoever does so destroys himself.

"Adultery is a sin that like ripples on the
water reverberates outward, touching many lives
more often than not, affecting generations."
~ Unknown

"When a man is faithful, there's nothing to
hide; he has no messages to delete."
~ Albert Amara

5

The Spirit of David's Adultery

❖ ❖

THE MAN AFTER GOD'S HEART

I'm a little bit saddened and with mixed feelings as I write about the beloved Psalmist, warrior and lover of God who God called "a man after my heart," in this way. To be honest, David was a righteous king and citizen that lived most of his life in the fear of his God, except for this little error in his life that stained part of his reputation, but it's always the little things that become big. Regardless of that, God called him a man after His heart, because he always sought after the will of God and wanted to be in right standing with His Maker. It's sad this happened to him because he took over the Kingdom at a time when Israel was lukewarm towards their God, because his predecessor and first king of Israel, Saul, had led the nation to that state. He defeated the giant Goliath when no one else had the courage to face him, including the most decorated soldier of that time, Saul. One thing noteworthy here is that Saul had a military presence, as the scriptures tell us in 1 Samuel 9:2 and 10:23; taller than everyone from his shoulder up. David on the other hand was not as intimidating as Saul but he had the most important thing of all and that was the presence of God. The Lord gave him victory over the giant and he took the shame and possible enslavement looming over Israel away.

I'm a bit saddened because there's no other individual God used those set of words for in His word "a man after my heart," except for David and we know God does not use words loosely. Unlike his predecessor Saul, David was humble, faithful, obedient, and repentant, devoted to and revered his God. Nevertheless, at a very unsuspecting time, he allowed this demon to lead him down the path of lust, adultery, deception, and murder. My focus is not on David, but on what that spirit that led him to commit this wickedness is capable of and how it attacks. After the iniquity, it tried to tarnish David's reputation (Proverbs 22:1) to the point that his son revolted against him and people felt it was warranted, because of the murder of Uriah, which David planned as a cover up for his infidelity. But, we see how God's mercy came into action for this man of God, as he was restored back to the throne as the king of Israel. This also goes to show us that we are not called to judge our leaders, but to pray for them. God's their judge, not us. So, as I write about this man of God, I realize that he was cleared of his wrong doing before God after repentance, so I'm not judging him, but exposing the tactics of the demon that led him down that dark alley.

ALWAYS FROM A POSITION OF HIGHER AUTHORITY

In 2 Samuel 11:2, the scripture states:

"Then it happened one evening that David arose from his bed and walked on the roof of the king's house. And from the roof he saw a woman bathing, and the woman was very beautiful to behold."

As we see in the above scripture, David was looking at this woman from a rooftop, or from a position of higher elevation. "Looking at Bathsheba from a rooftop" is a spiritual metaphor for the pride of men in this position, as they look at woman in lesser positions they desire to devour sexually. By all accounts, David was in a position of higher social status, or authority, compared to this woman. He was the king of Israel and also a prophet of God and to his credit, he had tried to restrain himself from using his position negatively, except on this one occasion and we all know that's all Satan needs - one opportunity. This demon tempted David to use that power that was so readily available to him to get his sexual urge satisfied, and he consented foolishly thinking it would only be a one-time fling. David acted stupidly, but that's what sin is "stupidity at its finest." Most, or maybe all, of the sexual misconducts revealed in 2017 (from Harvey Weinstein to the others) were of men in positions of power. The same demon that deceived David was the one operating in them.

While the demon of Potiphar's wife is a spirit using women to seduce men, this spirit of David's adultery is one that influences men to go after women of lesser position or power. It always operates from that elevated position of power, or pride, that sees its victims as trophies of its hard work (Ecclesiastes 2:10). Make no mistake about it; its goal is to defile your bed, whether you're married or not. It may come in the form of a male boss that promises an upcoming, unsuspecting female employee a promotion at the cost of sleeping with him. Sisters, please hear me; the person under the influence of this spirit may actually think they are doing nothing wrong, especially if they're not Christian, until they get caught. They may think one of the perks of being successful is to sleep with many beautiful and attractive women and that you're just one of the trophies on the shelf to grab. They actually believe "all game is fair until you get caught;" a lie that can only be sold by the master liar himself, Satan.

THE HOMEWORK

David could have simply walked down from the rooftop of his mansion, talked to Bathsheba and gotten all the info he needed from her without having anyone involved. Scripture tells us David saw that she was a very beautiful woman, so he must have been in close proximity to see the physical features of this woman, so why didn't he go down? It's a thing of pride and people in that position cannot risk being humiliated, as they have a reputation to uphold, even if it's a fake one. They have to do their homework first before they make their move, and David did that. He got her full genealogy and found out her husband was a captain in his army, giving him further reason to strike. He was now justified that even if he failed, it wouldn't look bad on him, as that would be the word of a lower official's wife over that of a king. Do you remember what we discussed in the earlier chapter of the word of the wife of Potiphar over that of Joseph's? It's the same concept here, and the unsuspecting Bathsheba had no clue what was coming to her.

When an influential man is seeking to be in your presence and knows all your likes and dislikes, don't be fooled. He probably has done his homework and knows a lot more about you than you think, so don't be so awestruck and passing out that he knows your favorite fragrance in perfumes and your favorite food joints. You need discernment of the Spirit to know the fake from the real and this is especially so for single ladies; married ladies, you know you should not even entertain that conversation, but knowing the devil, he's going to try anyway. As a famous writer puts it, men on the prowl can be divided into two groups: dogs and snakes. A dog has to eat every day, so it goes after everything edible. On the other hand, the snake does not have to eat every day, so it is very patient and studies the habits of its prey to know when to strike. The homework, or research, is the process of waiting and studying your habits, likes and dislikes. You may think he's a gentleman, but you may be the subject of his study. Watch out and pray for discernment.

THE EMOTIONAL ATTACHMENT

David had an emotional attachment to this woman and wanted her to be his wife. There are two things that clearly prove this in the text (2 Samuel 11). The first was the fact that he was willing to kill Uriah to take his wife. He followed that plan through, carrying it out with Uriah being the messenger of the news of his own execution without even the slightest clue of the king's salacious plan. David betrayed Uriah's trust but as a loyal soldier, Uriah was obedient to the point of death and whenever that happens, God takes up the case of the one wronged. But, maybe you may say "Nah! He was just trying to cover up his sin." Let's look at the second one and in this, we see that after the death of Uriah, David sent and took his wife to be his, of course after her mourning period, but how long was her mourning period? The normal time for this period of mourning was thirty days and was called the "Shloshim" in the Hebrew. But why couldn't the king wait longer? The reason is the emotional attachment; this lady was etched in the recesses of David's soul and he could not get her out of his mind, so he took her as his wife immediately after the mourning period.

Ladies, be very careful when you start getting emotionally connected to someone you know you shouldn't be connected to, either because they're married or you're married, or they're already attached to someone else. Most of the time, our conscience will give us an indication that we're stepping out of the will of God, after we've ignored the Word of God or His Spirit's warnings. God uses our conscience as a back up to His warnings. Truthfully, the emotional attachment is one of the hardest to break. A one-night stand is wrong and many married people have committed this act of betrayal and have been reconciled back to their spouses, but David's adultery was more than a one night stand. When emotions are involved, the person gets stuck in your subconscious and you cannot get them out of there without the power of the Holy Spirit in Jesus' name. If you're a married woman and are emotionally attached to someone else, sex will not even be pleasurable with your spouse, because your mind is with someone else. You need to break that emotional bond in the name of Jesus and start speaking to your soul to respond to your mate.

BATHSHEBA'S 1st ERROR: CARELESSNESS

Now, we all know it takes two to tangle, so totally acquitting Bathsheba of all wrongs in this act would make us totally gullible to a lie, indeed. While many preachers accuse this woman of seducing the king of Israel, I see something different and that first mistake was carelessness. It was Spring and she knew it was the time kings go out to battle; she must have known because her husband was not home, having left with the king's army. She may have also lived close by the palace and of course in those days, there were no indoor bathrooms; people took baths in a river/brook, so she went to the one closest to their house, which happened to be by the king's palace. She assumed no one was home, since the men were out fighting, so she let down her guard and did something that should only be done in private, bathe herself while it was still visible outside. The only problem on that day was that she didn't know the king was home and of course, after his front seat row inspection of her body, he sent for her and had sex with her. While it's abundantly clear that David was the perpetrator of this crime, Bathsheba could have been more discreet.

Before someone accuses me of taking the blame off David and shaming this woman, fast forward to today and take a look at ladies in charismatic churches, see what they wear. Many women, especially in the summer time have their clothes hugging them so tight and cleavage so revealing, that you can't tell the difference between them and those that don't know God. Honestly, we know it's hot out there and some don't see a problem with this, but when you look at it, there's no other word to describe it but *carelessness*. No one is saying you have to wear bags to cover up because no matter what you wear, a man full of lust will undress you with his eyes, but please don't make it easy for these men. It's your responsibility to dress modestly, so you don't draw negative sexual attention to yourself (1 Timothy 2:9). Some women, on the other hand, love that type of attention and truthfully, many have not been mentored by older, wiser women, so they don't know how to dress. But please hear me, if everything is hanging loosely and you love it when heads turn your way because of your hot body, you're no longer walking in love. The simple truth is that while women are triggered sexually by touch, men are triggered by sight, but of course, you knew that.

BATHSHEBA'S 2nd ERROR: STARSTRUCK

When you read this story of David and Bathsheba, you can't help to think and ask yourself, "Why didn't Bathsheba just say no like Joseph did?" To give my perspective on that, I'll use a popular line you probably have heard used and that is, "I'm faithful to my spouse with the exception of this celebrity." Even though it's used as a joke by many, it's so much in their subconscious that they might follow through if the situation presents itself. Here was this woman who was the wife of a captain in Israel (Uriah was one of David's thirty mightiest men) who didn't know she was in the thoughts of the highest authority figure in Israel, being pursued by him. She was "startruck" and in that, she faltered and sinned. God didn't call us to worship celebrities or famous people, but Him alone. Of course, David had the greater sin (if there was ever a scale to measure sin) because he initiated it, but she could have stopped it by refusing the offer. We should not fear anyone to the point that we sin against our God; that will be the fear of man, which is as wrong as worshipping an idol.

Don't you ever think: what would have happened if she had just said "no?" I think she would have snapped the king back to his senses and preserved the name of the house of David from the shame of adultery, cover up, murder, and even civil war where David's wives were sexually violated by his son, Absalom. She may have thought, "Oh, it's just one night, I'll never do it again," but it ended up with her being pregnant and David committing murder to cover his sin. That same spirit is operating today in a different setting, but the tactics have not changed. Every now and again, we'll hear a story of a sexual scandal involving a man of high reputation (like the ones we're hearing of in this year, 2017), getting sexually involved with a younger woman, and you can't help but think why people don't learn from history. While it's true that a lot of younger women love the attention, fame, money, and power this relationship gives them, we have to also realize that some are too awestruck to resist the temptation. Just like Bathsheba, some Christian women don't even realize the beauty, grace, and favor they possess just because they grew up in church all their lives and no one ever complimented them for those things.

Ladies, Satan knows those qualities are very rare among his children, so he sends men of influence after you to extinguish that glow on you. Men, under the control of the spirit of David's adultery, are attracted to women that possess these qualities because for them, it's not only about the sex, but also how you make them feel about themselves. Most of them have wives who have become hardened by the attitudes of these same men, so your gentleness and grace is very attractive to them; it reminds them of a younger version of them and as you may know, everyone wants to stay young. I see it here a lot in Germany in the church I pastor.

Some young lady starts coming to church and the glow of God in and on her makes her look so attractive and men that had dumped her start getting attracted to her. She does not know the difference and falls for the bait. After a while when you see her, she's not the same because the fire has been extinguished. Ladies, please don't fall prey to such temptations and please don't be *starstruck*. The power is in your hands and God can use you to bring about a change in that person tempting you.

HELP! MY SPOUSE DOESN'T TURN ME ON ANYMORE

Maybe you've overcome the spirits I spoke of in the last chapter and this one, but are no longer sexually attracted to your spouse and this my friend is a hidden and growing problem in many households. Many have quit watching porn or having extramarital affairs and are now trying to please their spouse, but they find that the man/woman they should spend the rest of their lives with is not fulfilling them sexually, so they start looking outside of their marriages for that sexual pleasure. I used to wonder why some older, good looking women were drawn to younger men in their prime (I know this because I had those advances from some ladies too as a younger man), but I now know the answer. Most of these women have husbands who are no longer sexually active, either because of a physical injury or lack of interest. Basically, their naked bodies no longer woo their hubbies, but these are the same men that will come alive in the presence of another woman.

PLEASE DON'T RESORT TO THIS: In October 2017, CNN did an article entitled: "The Changing Reasons Why Women Cheat on Their Husbands" and it is really sad to hear the reasons.

The cheating behavior that was long accepted as a male prerogative is now spreading amongst married women, but this is why God has anointed me to write this book; together we can bring awareness to the masses and stop this evil. It is pretty obvious that most of these women aren't Christian, because they looked at the institution of marriage as restricting and suffocating, instead of a blessing. Trust me, I know marriage can be challenging, but we are not alone, as we have the Holy Spirit on our side to help us, but that teaching is for another book. The main reason for having extramarital affairs among these women is boredom; oh it gets better! They're looking for new ways to stay in their present marriages, as they don't want a divorce or separation, because of their bitter experiences as a child of divorced parents.

One woman recalled her most vivid memory of Christmas and it was of her parents driving in the blizzard and parking on the side of I-95 highway for her and her brother to be given to one of her parents, so they can spend Christmas with the parent whose turn it was, without either exchanging a word. Because they want to prevent such experiences from re-occurring, they find a sexual mate other than their husbands to spice things up and infidelity becomes a drug for the boredom of marriage. There are even websites created exclusively for cheaters that want to keep their infidelities private but for some women, there's little secrecy or shame about their sexual adventures because for them, it is a way of keeping them from a bitter divorce. Some think their husbands know, but choose to look the other way. Even though that topic is for another book, but who says marriage has to be boring? The Holy Spirit wants to help you. Ask Him!

A HUGE REASON FOR THE SHRINKING LIBIDO

If you have Jesus in your heart and are trying to live right but find that the thrill in your marriage bed is gone, please stay faithful to the Lord and don't do anything that will invite demons into your bed to defile it; definitely don't go outside to have it satisfied. Ladies, there's something you have to understand when your man's libido, which was formerly very active, suddenly goes south, especially if he's in his prime. First of all, if he loves you and wants to please His God (especially if he just accepted the Lord), please know he feels bad about it and useless in bed with you. But, maybe the most important thing you need to know is that most likely the reason for the shrinking libido is that the thrill of the illegal sex that used to arouse him, either through masturbation or other women, is gone. This here is huge and should not be downplayed, because it can affect his professional, as well as his private life. Most men that lose their sex drive feel useless to their wives and it can have a psychological effect on them that will drive down their productivity in every area of their life.

We all know of story of the golfer who was ranked no.1 and was revered in his sport as the best finisher. I'm only using his story as an example of what the Holy Spirit taught me in this area, not to judge him and you won't see this on any news magazine. After his infidelities came out in 2009, he has not won a major golf championship since; I'm rooting for that to change. The question has been asked many times over: what happened to golf's golden boy? Many said it's because of the death of his dad, but after his dad died, he won couple of majors. As long as his sexual transgressions were presumably under covers and he had the image of the perfect family man, he did well and wowed the sports world, but when it became public, it seemed the fuel that kept him going was yanked away and the injuries kicked in. I'm not saying he's been faithful ever since, but something happened there that took the edge away. In my opinion, he was now under the watchful eye of the media and the entire sports world, and was now forced to play by the rules. That was boring, and it affected his profession.

Now, compare that to your hubby who's trying to do the right thing and make love to the love of his life – you. If he's been used to pleasuring himself with other women, toys, or videos, you are boring because he's not used to that; he has to focus extremely hard, especially now that he knows it's sinful to think of others when he's with you. That's the reason he's not interested in sex with you, but please don't walk away from him now, especially so if he's working at this; he has to re-learn sex the right way. This issue is very important and unless both of you work on this together, it can lead to separation, which is what Satan wants. The enemy is trying to get him to revert to his old habits, which will be disastrous to your marriage, so don't be upset or frustrated. My advice: be patient with him, don't judge, but above all, ask Holy Spirit for help. He wants to help! I believe we underestimate the help of the Holy Spirit. You don't need any tutorials here; He created sex and it's not an unholy thing to ask Him for help in this area. 1 John 2:27 says you don't need any one teach you, but the anointing in you will teach and that includes sex!

FAITHFULNESS STARTS WITH CHRIST

Would you try to attend lectures in a University you're not en-rolled in or try to teach a college course with no education? Probably not and that's because you've not met the requirements to carry out those actions, which is to enroll in the school or become a university lecturer first, respectively. Likewise, to be sexually pure, you'll need the One who commanded us to keep our beds pure to help you, and it's no other but the man Jesus Christ who is also God, and that's who these powerful men caught up in sex scandals need. So right now, if you haven't accepted Jesus Christ as your Lord and Savior, please sincerely pray this powerful prayer from your heart: Say this prayer out loud right now:

"Dear God, I want to be a part of Your family. You said in Your Word that if I acknowledge that You raised Jesus from the dead, and that I accept Him as my Lord and Savior, I would be saved. So God, I now say that I believe You raised Jesus from the dead and that He is alive and well. I accept Him now as my personal Lord and Savior. I accept my salvation from sin right now. I am now saved. Jesus is my Lord. Jesus is my Savior. Thank You, Father God, for forgiving me, saving me, and giving me eternal life with You. In Jesus name Amen!"

One thing that happens to people that want to stay sexually pure and they don't understand is sexual dreams. If this happens, don't despair. What's happening is that since you willingly stopped donating your semen to the devil, he's mad and wants it back, so he starts manifesting himself in dreams. Whenever it happens, come against that spirit in Jesus' name but more importantly, bring this to the court of heaven (Zechariah 3:1-4) and tell the Lord you want a divorce from this sexual demon. You'll find out that it will eventually stop but even if it happens again, take it back to God and don't give up, because it will surely stop. Also, please know that we have to be faithful to Christ first before any spouse, so even if you never get sexually fulfilled here on earth ever again, but stay faithful to the Lord, it's worth it. Heaven is worth the sacrifice and you'll not be disappointed. When you think of it, no matter how great the sex is, we are still flesh and blood and when we die, our bodies can't do the things we so craved for and got us into sin here on earth. There's no sex in heaven because we will be married to the Lord, so be faithful to Him. However, while we are here on earth, we have a helper in the Holy Spirit that can bring the thrill back into our marriage beds and all we have.

CHAPTER 6
ENEMY AT THE GATES

Nehemiah 4:6
So we built the wall and the whole wall was joined together to half its height, for the people had a mind to work. (NASB)

"When an enemy can't penetrate your walls, he comes as a friend bringing gifts."
~ Albert Amara

6

Enemy at the Gates

※ ※

WHY BUILD A WALL/GATE?

In Bible days and before the invention of the airplane and weapons of mass destruction, the construction of a physical wall with gates was very instrumental to the security of a nation or city. A wall and its gates went together in ancient times and without a good wall, the gates were useless. The walls of Jerusalem and China are good examples, to name a few. The wall provided security and protection from invaders and enemies all around, and the gates were the only points of entry and were most of the time guarded by guards. Today, it's impractical to build a wall to protect against rockets and airplane missiles, so many countries don't have a physical wall. No country has the physical resources or man power to build a 40,000 feet or 7.5 mile high wall, but that doesn't mean the sovereign boundaries of a nation should not be protected anymore. Today, nations spend billions of dollars on national defense every year for that purpose, to improve their missile and radar technology, so their walls won't be breached by enemies. Believers, it's no different for the Christian, because we are a city and the enemy is fighting to re-enter his once controlled territory.

In the constant battle for your soul, you are that city and the enemy is trying all he can to breach your walls. The wall is the defense you put up against the world and Satan's tactics to enter the city and it comes by renewing your daily walk with the Lord. God, in turn, becomes a wall of protection around us (Proverbs 18:10; Job 1:10). The enemy knows your walls are impenetrable as long as you stay in God and He (God) in you, so he tries to enter through the gates, because he knows they are the only way he can enter. He bombards the gates daily with temptations in the hopes that you'll give in and open one of them; he knows he cannot force God out, so he tempts you to open the ports of entry. When one of those gates is open, the city becomes vulnerable and the merciless onslaught resumes. They are the eye, ear, nose, mouth, and the touch, or feel, gates. Let's go through each one in the context of sexual sin. It's not to say other sins are unimportant, but as this book is about sexual purity, I want to focus on sexual sins, because dealing with other transgressions will take the focus off of what the Holy Spirit is saying here. I also believe God wants to handle this issue of sexual purity in the US and around the world now.

THE EYE GATE

Men typically open this gate, as we can undress a woman with her clothes on just by staring. When I was in the Army, we would have company, platoon, or squad runs and during those runs, I would be so tempted to look at the jiggling bodies of female soldiers to the point of lust. Since I knew the Word of God, sometimes I would glance a couple of times, but that would be enough to do the damage. You may say, "That's nothing, everyone's done that." I know that and I've heard ladies talk of the fantasies they had of other male soldiers, as well. However, this attitude if left unchecked, can lead anyone to a dark place they never intended to be in. Many crimes such as rape, murder, and necrophilia start from this unchecked desire; it fans itself into a raging wild fire. I'm reminded of a statement my leaders in the Army used a lot when I was a junior soldier and that is, "A whole bunch of unclassified material can be pieced together to uncover a classified document."

We as children of God have to remember that the eyes are a gate, and that it's the enemy's favorite gate. For me, when once those pictures had entered my mind (sometimes, it's just an attractive young woman walking and minding her business), they will stay there, until I watch porn or masturbate. They're like the unclassified materials my leaders were talking about and they etch in your soul, until the whole picture forms and drive you to sin. Today, a lot of young people are being deceived to think that they can allow R rated or even PG-13 movies and other pictures classified as *soft porn* through the eye gate, because of their classified ratings. They let their guards down thinking they're now mature and that gates are for baby Christians, not knowing that a *spy* is loose in the city.

Satan hates walls; he says, "Let down the walls and open the gates and let's all have one big family," but that's how he got Eve to eat the fruit, Aachen to steal the things devoted to God, and how he wanted our Lord to sin by eating the bread after forty days of fasting. Would you allow a known registered sex offender to watch your kids while you go on a month long vacation? No one in his/her right mind would, because they know exactly what will happen. Rather, if you see this person within close proximity of your house, you'll alert the authorities. Why don't we do the same with the images we allow in the city God's given us to guard? What we fail to realize is that sin is seeking to oust our King (Jesus Christ) and sit on the throne of our hearts. You think that's impossible? Just remember this: the access through the gates of the city and permission of who sits as King is only given through our consent. The pictures that come through our eyes always present the images to be better than they actually are, and sin comes hidden as one of the *good guys*, but its purpose is to open the other gates, so the enemy can overrun the city. Those that have fallen to sexual sins will tell you the despicable things they did, even as a child of God when they let open the *eye gate*; the enemy came in and opened the other gates, and they got into other sinful acts.

THE EAR GATE

There's a popular scripture in Romans 10:17 many Christians quote: *"So then faith comes by hearing, and hearing by the word of God."*

The first thing that ever happened in our world was a sound wave spoken by our God to produce light and by doing that, God instituted a principle that we can create by sound. When Satan entered the earth, he copied that as he always does; he's not a creator just a very good copy machine, so the first recorded thing he did was speak. He spoke words that had an ambiguous meaning to the woman, instead of words of faith which she was used to, as they had a direct and singular meaning. This shows that as the hearing of faith-filled words produces faith, so likewise the continual hearing of words of sexual lust will lead you down to the path of sin. Many Christians, especially singles, listen to romantic love songs that simply heighten their sexual desires and wonder why they can't get rid of lustful thoughts. The answer is simple: you've left the *ear gate* open and now an enemy is inside the city trying to open the other gates. It will succeed in its mission if you continue giving the excuse of "Oh, it's just a song," or "I grew up listening to them and I love the way they make me feel."

I had a buddy in the Army whose marriage ended up in a divorce, because he cheated and even though I don't know the details of the breakup, the above were his excuses for listening to those types of songs. Words are very powerful, especially when they are accompanied with music. They have the ability to put you in the right mood to sin and when once you're there, those feelings of "the good old days" come rushing back and the things you never thought you'd ever do again become quite easy to do. That's why if you don't want to commit adultery/fornication with that old girlfriend, you have to stop listening to those songs that the two of you used to enjoy together before you knew Christ. Those songs act as a bridge and can re-connect the two of you at any time. Many dates end up with sex being involved, because of carefully selected songs targeted at stimulating that pleasure chemical, dopamine, in the unsuspecting one. The same thing happens when you join those conversations about sexual exploits. Before you know it, you'll be asking, "How did I get here?" (Psalm 1:1-3) Answer is simple: You left open the *ear gate* and now an enemy is in the city. So, guard that *ear gate* because if faith comes by hearing, so can lust, as well.

NOSE GATE

I once gave a lady a hug and she told me, "I love men that use good cologne." I was shocked by her reaction, as I was not wearing cologne but a nice smelling body spray, but this was a "turn on" for this lady, as I later found out. From my various observations, I'll make a bold statement here and that is if the *eye gate* and *ear gate* openers are typically men, the ones that mostly fall to the bait of opening the *nose gate* are typically women, (I may stand corrected). It's been scientifically proven that women have a stronger and better sense of smell than men; I personally think that's why ladies appreciate flowers better than men. Brazilian researchers found out that on average, women have 43% more cells than men in their olfactory bulbs – the region that controls smell in the brain. Ladies, watch out for this when you start to like a workmate/colleague's cologne more than usual. It may be the enemy bombarding your *nose gate* so you can open it, be aware of that tactic. Sometimes, men including myself, wear a body spray innocently just to smell good, but there are some that know the exact type and amount (not too much and not too little) to wear to get a woman's attention.

In 1 Corinthians 8:13, Paul states that we should be careful that the exercise of our rights doesn't cause another to stumble. He goes on to say in verse 13 of the same chapter that if meat causes his brother/sister to sin, he won't eat it anymore. Now, that was meat which is essential to our survival and most people today will blame the person being tempted of being weak in faith, but that's how spiritually mature Paul was. Paul understood a spiritual principle many of us have neglected today and that is when you do anything that causes anyone to stumble, you sin against Christ. Of course, many of us that dress well and wear nice smelling fragrances don't do it to cause people to fall into sin, but if that's your motive brother/sister, you're no longer waking in love (Romans 14:15). I'll boldly say to you as Paul said in Romans 14:15 about food, "If your brother or sister is tempted by your fragrance (even if it's a nice smelling one that you paid a lot of money for) but you refuse to stop using it, you're no longer walking in love. I know not everyone can receive this, but it is the gospel truth and it is called *spiritual responsibility* for our neighbor."

THE MOUTH GATE

Ha! The *mouth gate*, that's one interesting one. Most people don't understand how you can be tempted by your mouth, as this is a gate that seems very unlikely to fall to temptation. You don't use your mouth to look at nude pictures nor do you listen to sexually laced lyrics with it, right? Sounds fair enough and by the look of things, it seems only a person who doesn't care about his/her sexual purity will open this gate willingly. However, let's not forget that we have an adversary (who cannot out smart us, as we have the Holy One inside us) who needless to say, is very tricky. He comes through this gate mostly by way of the feel, or touch, gate, although he can use other gates. You may ask, "How does he do that?" Thanks for asking. Have you heard people say things like "Hmm…hmm…hmm, the things I'll do to her if I was not married?"

That's an imagination of the heart that has now become strong enough to be voiced out through the *mouth gate* and if that person doesn't change that confession; he/she will carry out that imagination. That's why we should protect this gate, because just as Proverbs 18:7 tells us, a fool's mouth can put him in a trap.

An experiment was done by the late Japanese researcher Masaru Emoto on the effect of sound on water and the results were amazing. Sound turns energy and matter into forms; water is no different, as it absorbs and stores sound effects; what you give out is what you create. He froze glass bottles of water in a jar and then observed the molecular structure formed when left overnight under a dark field microscope that had photographic capabilities. On one jar he typed the words "thank you" and on another he typed the words "you make me sick, I will kill you." The structure of the water in the jar with the words "thank you" formed beautiful snow flake crystals and those with the words "you make me sick, I will kill you," were distorted. Now. if you don't know let me inform you that thoughts are powerful; they are words in unspoken form and that's what the experiment demonstrated. Even though Mr. Emoto didn't speak the words to the different jars, his intention of thought was communicated and they received the message and acted accordingly.

The body of a mature human consists of over 70% of water and about that same percentage of water covers our planet. God made us out of the dust of the earth, which makes us *earth men*, so when you speak negatively to yourself with words such as "I can't seem to overcome this porn addiction," or "I have a weakness for women with big butts," you're deforming your crystals and making it impossible to overcome that sexual addiction. The elements inside you will listen and obey whatever command given to them. Most Christians have been unsaved for more years than they've been saved and so they have been thinking and speaking negatively for more years of their lives than they've been speaking positively, presumably. Therefore, the balance of power is naturally on the negative, but it can be shifted back to the positive, or how God intended it to be by speaking words of faith backed up with God's Word. Every learned negative word, or habit, can be unlearned by replacing it with God's Word. Remember, the mission is to shut the *mouth gate*.

THE FEEL GATE (TOUCH GATE)

John has been counseling Jennifer, a young Christian lady, at work. She's a young believer and has been having problems with her spouse, so since there are no other serious Christians in the office, she opened up to John, and he's been helping her with scripture verses and words of encouragement. Lately, John has been growing fond of the daily morning meetings with Jennifer and waits in anticipation at their usual place of meeting just before work resumes; the only problem is that John's wife knows nothing of Jennifer. Today, she cried on his shoulder and her perfume reminded him of the days he and his wife just met and started dating. He's given ladies other than his wife hugs before, but this felt different, as it lasted a little longer and the thought of a younger woman in his arms this way, gave him a sense of guilty pleasure. After the hug, he offered to hold her hand and walked with her for a brief moment to assure her of his support, but he knew he was now treading on dangerous grounds and an invisible line of no return was not far from that point. John knows one thing, he has a decision to make; both continue on in this path and cross that line, or calmly, but firmly, tell Jennifer they have to stop seeing each other, as both are married.

John and Jennifer are under enemy attack at the *feel gate* (touch gate) and the barrage of fire will only intensify if they don't do something to stop it. The enemy will always resort to attack this gate after he's failed to enter through other gates and to my estimation, that's because this gate is the nervous system of the senses. It is the central processing center of all other senses, or gates. Without the participation of the *feel gate* (touch gate), temptation does not make sense, because it won't be beneficial, or pleasurable to the senses. We see this in Genesis 3:6; sin entered Eve through the *eye gate*, but it had to be approved by the *feel gate* (touch gate) because the verse said that when the woman saw that the tree was one to be desired to make one wise, she took and ate it. She desired, or rather had a strong craving, longing, or yearning (these are all nouns for strong feeling) for the tree and so opened the *feel gate* (touch gate). This is why a woman can forgive her husband for a one night stand, but will ask the question: "Do you love her?" (The other woman.)

And of course that is vice versa, because when a spouse finds out his/her partner's feelings for them are compromised, they know it isn't healthy to stay in that relationship.

Most don't know this gate is constantly under attack by the enemy and keep on blaming themselves for their failures. Ephesians 6:16 tells us exactly how Satan does this:

"In addition to all this, take up the shield of faith, with which you can extinguish all the flaming arrows of the evil one."

Those thoughts bombarding your mind of you having a fling with your neighbor's young wife that seemed to come out of nowhere are not your own. They are carefully designed arrows sent against your soul because since you were in the devil's camp before, he knows your habits, your likes, and dislikes. He knows you love red, blonde, or black haired women with an athletic build and she fits that category, so that's why he sent that particular arrow to your soul. In John and Jennifer's case, those arrows were sent to both of them, as demons can work on two people to accomplish the same destructive end at this gate. If they don't use the weapons provided to them in Ephesians 6, they'll end up having not only consensual sex, but a consensual breakup from their spouses.

But there's good news: whether you're wrestling with the spirit of Potiphar's wife, that of David's adultery, or that of LGBT and you're confused about your sexuality, please realize one thing and that is they are all fallen spirits and the bigger the giant, the greater the fall. As one of my pastors used to say, "The demons in the higher echelon of command are the ones that are easiest to deal with, because they understand authority better."

The same strategy David used to defeat that giant Goliath, is the same we are going to use to defeat these demons of lust, but please don't stop here. Let's go on to the last chapter of this revelation: Christ Consciousness.

CHAPTER SEVEN
CHRIST CONSCIOUSNESS

2 Peter 3:18
But grow in the grace and knowledge of our Lord and Savior Jesus Christ. To Him be glory both now and forever! Amen.

"You don't need to make Christ famous; He already is. He created everything while you were just a thought in His mind, without your help. What you need to do is grow in His consciousness." ~Albert Amara

7

Christ Consciousness

✦ ✦

WHAT IS CHRIST CONSCIOUSNESS?

If you're like me you may be asking, "I've read six chapters of information on the effects of sexual sin, so how do I get out of it, or have a pleasurable sexual experience with my spouse with a clear conscience? Glory to God and congratulations! You stuck with me till the last chapter, so I want to personally thank you for that. The answer to your question is summarized in the heading of this chapter: "Christ Consciousness." Christ consciousness is the amount of knowledge of the Son of God (Jesus Christ) an individual knows that will allow that person to walk in total freedom and dominion in any area of his/her life. There are many paths to so-called "freedom" from all types of addictions taught by many philosophers and free thinkers, but there's only one true way with zero side effects and 100% satisfaction guaranteed, both in this world and in the world to come. That way is through Jesus Christ and I'm not talking of only salvation of the soul. Christ Consciousness is the knowledge of the Spirit of Jesus Christ made alive in your spirit man. It is having the same mind as Jesus Christ our Lord and walking in that same dominion and authority He walked in on earth and now in heaven.

Whatever Jesus did wasn't done in a vacuum, but was done openly for everyone to see and document. Whenever He cast out demons, it wasn't done in a spiritual clinic, but openly in front of everyone, so all could see. There was a reason for that and that reason was to show everyone how weak demons really are and that none could withstand His power, because He operated from a higher level of authority, or consciousness. Most importantly, He proved that what He was doing, His disciples and anyone who believed in Him, could do also. Knowing such authority and power, Paul cautions us in Philippians 2:5-7 to have the mindset of Christ who, though He was God, did not consider it a thing He could take advantage of. Instead, He humbled Himself to the level of a servant and served those He came to die for, even though He created them. This is so important; that's why Peter tells us in his 2nd epistle, chapter 3 verse 18, to grow in the knowledge and grace of Christ and that's *Christ consciousness*. With the amount of power and authority we possess, if we're not careful, we could be prideful and refuse to serve. But, God's power in us is only displayed in the place and with an attitude of servitude.

WHAT IT'S NOT

A lot of celebrities and public figures are increasingly flocking to and embracing a movement they call "Christ consciousness." They claim it's helping them connect with their deeper essence to achieve true peace, meaning, and purpose for their lives. Believers, be aware because the Bible tells us that even Satan masquerades as an angel of light (2 Corinthians 11:14). This type of *Christ consciousness* gives an earthly type of peace, but it is in exchange for the souls of those that believe and practice its demonic teachings. It is not of or from our God, nor does it have anything in it that exalts our Lord Jesus Christ; rather, it is a rebrand of Eastern mysticism. They have hijacked the name "Christ" which is from the Greek "Christos," meaning the anointed One for their selfish motives. On their website, the Center for Christ Consciousness teaches that *Christ consciousness* is the "highest state of intellectual development, emotional balance, and spiritual maturity…" and that Jesus Himself achieved it, that's why He was given the title "Christ." As expected, every religion is welcome and can attain this "Christed" state of being. WHAT AN ABOMINATION!!!

This is why you have to know the Word of God and test the spirit in any movement to see whether it is of God, or from the enemy. On the Christ Consciousness website, they throw around buzz words like "God, divine, creator, child of God" and many more to give their religion a blanket appearance of the true God, Yahweh. When you pull back the covers and look beneath the surface, you'll see that it's full of dead bones and rotten flesh. This religion leads to one definite end, hell fire, because the only capable of giving true peace both on earth and in the world to come is Jesus Christ. When talking to proponents of the so-called *Christ Consciousness*, make sure you use the name of Jesus Christ over and over and tell them that's the only true consciousness you'd like to be under. 1 John 4:4 tells us that anyone that does not believe that Jesus has come in the flesh is not of God and to clarify that in verse 6 of the same chapter, it says we are of God and anyone who's of God hears our message and anyone who's not of God will not hear our message. God further debunks their message by adding that anyone who does not receive our message is of the spirit of error. Their type of *Christ consciousness* is of the spirit of error and will not accept the true message of our Messiah.

CONSCIOUSNESS OF WE ARE FROM ABOVE

We were in the mind of God ages before anyone of us was born; therefore, we came from above, where the "Most High" God dwells. Ephesians 2: 5, 6 tells us that while we were in our sins, God made us alive with Christ and raised us together with Him and not only that, but He seated us together with Him and the purpose is to rule with Him. Since we are seated with and in Christ, Ephesians 1: 20, 21 tells us our position in heaven is with Him on the right hand of God and far above any principality and power, might, dominion, and any name under heaven. According to 2 Corinthians 12:2, we know there are three heavens and they are:

❖ The 1st heaven, otherwise known as our atmosphere, is about 300 miles (480 Km) thick.

❖ The 2nd heaven which is also known as space, but most importantly, where demons dwell (Ephesians 2:1, 2; Ephesians 6:12). This is so vast that scientists say the distance from earth to the farthest object is 13 billion years light years away; it is mind-boggling.

❖ The 3rd heaven is where almighty God dwells. No human mind can fathom that distance. No telescope has even seen the outskirts of this heavenly city.

This is where God says you're seated with Christ, far above the second heaven where Satan's demons reside. There's a reason our God is called the Most High God and that's because no one is higher than Him whether in altitude, authority, or in power. I don't under-estimate the fact that the devil has very strong demons in hierarchical order, but they are only strong when we compare them to our own might. We are nothing without our God, so when He says as Jesus is right now, so are we in this world (1 John 4:17), that's exactly what He means. We have the same authority, power, and dominion Jesus has right now in heaven, so no matter the hierarchy of the demon, it is subject to us in Jesus' name. We have to have that same consciousness Christ has for us to reign over any addiction.

CONSCIOUSNESS OF NO FEAR FOR SIN

Most people bound in sexual sins keep falling into the same habit, because of the fear of the sin. That's because fear is negative worship and anything you worship, you will fall under the power of. 1 John 4:18 shows us that fear has torment and it's because of the punishment it brings with it. I know most people don't see the fear of sin as worship, but look on the opposite side of that fear and think of how you worship God. You have a holy reverence for Him born out of love, so you bow down to Him. With sin, you have a negative reverence for the fear of not obeying your feelings and what it can escalate to, so you bow down every time to that demon, until deliverance comes. Instead of resisting the urge, people masturbate because they don't want the built up pressure to lead them to worse things, but they fail to realize that if they make it a habit of resisting, they will get stronger and defeat the habit.

Make no mistake about it, it's an invitation to worship but unfortunately, it's not the Most High God they're bowing down to, but a demon. Most addicts will tell you they can't help it and I believe it because by this time, it has become a stronghold that only the Lord can break.

Oh how sad to keep falling into the same addictions you hate so much! I've been there and so have many: closed every door to that addiction (threw away all the porn books, videos, and paraphernalia); been clean for half a year, but then that thought mixed with old feelings drops on you and your heart starts racing. You want to honor God, but you're so paralyzed by the fear of falling that you freeze up and end up falling again. That spirit, in turn, wraps its grip tighter and tighter (like the coils of a constrictor on its prey) on the mind of the prisoner until it becomes a stronghold, all the while telling you it's hopeless to try and get free. It took me too long to realize this, but that's when you should realize you're dealing with a giant. As I said in the last chapter, there's one thing I learned from David's account of dealing with Goliath and that is giants go down easily, but you cannot use their weapons or fight them on their turf. You have to stop the vicious cycle of fear and recognize the consciousness of Christ available to you in this area. Switch to the consciousness of LOVE.

CONSCIOUSNESS OF LOVE

God never told us to fear sin, particularly sexual immorality. He told us to run away from it –1 Corinthians 6:18– which is another way of saying "have nothing to do with it." The only One He told us to fear in His Word is Him. As simple as it sounds, Love is the answer to your addiction problem. It was Love that conquered the grave while we all stood condemned awaiting hell's fury. Love reached down to hell, took its keys and authority, and has made it available to the least of the saints. My friend, Love is not just an emotion; but is God Himself – 1 John 4:16– and is the neutralizer to all of Satan's venom. When you understand the power of God's Love for you, you'll be so overwhelmed that it will overcome your fear of sin and it'll just eat up your desire for it – sin. We have overcome every demon, including the chief himself, Satan, because the greater One lives inside us. There's no weapon greater than Love and the devil has nothing in his arsenal to combat it. You have to understand Love before you understand the next thing we'll talk about: GRACE

CONCIOUSNESS OF CHRIST'S GRACE

Have you ever seen an eagle flying or a fish swimming? Does that eagle struggle to fly or does the fish gasp for air and move about awkwardly in the water? The answer is an emphatic, NO! That's because they are in their respective habitats and doing what they've been graced to do, and it's so beautiful to see them move. Likewise, you are in your supernatural habitat called Christ and *grace* is supplied (1 Timothy 1:14), as long as you stay in Him. So, why are you still pacing the floor, taking cold showers, and fighting with every ounce of your being when you get tempted? You actually look like a non-swimmer trying to swim, but fighting the water to stay afloat. We all know what happens to that type of swimmer; if he/she is not helped, they will eventually go under for good and drown. If you're in Christ, *grace* has been supplied for your freedom. You're like a V8, 1200 –horse power engine race car in a race with regular automobiles. Sit back, drive the car, and allow the gracefulness of the engine to bring you the win; your competition doesn't stand a chance. Basically, allow *grace* to fight for you. Most say they have to fight the devil calling it *spiritual warfare*, but spiritual combat is not fighting Satan; it's living in the victory God gave to us through Christ Jesus. I've noticed from scripture and everyday life that it's the small things that make a great difference in life, so stop seeing sexual addiction as a giant you can't defeat. It will fall just as Goliath fell before David weaponizing a small stone.

To put it in practical terms, let me explain how you defeat that addiction: when tempted and you feel like you're about to go down that path of defeat once again, simply surrender (I, most of the time, get on my knees, but it's not mandatory) to the power of God's *grace* and thank the Lord for the victory, which is in His *grace*. Remember, His *grace* never left, even though you felt weak. If you do this sincerely, with childlike faith, it is like a man finally stopping the action of fighting the water and relaxing in it. When God sees that His power goes into action, you'll never fall again. His Word says His everlasting hands are underneath (Deuteronomy 33:27). Psychologists say it takes a minimum of twenty-one days to break a habit and as long as sixty-six to form a new one, so I recommend you start today and don't take your foot off the pedal. Each day of victory adds to your confidence and before long, you'll be mentoring others. So, I'm not even going to subscribe to your fear of falling, because you won't and that's not fiction. As simple as it is, it is very powerful and will never fail. This is why Paul always never ends his letters without mentioning the *grace* of God; it is the power of God made available to us.

THE CONSCIOUSNESS OF SETTING YOUR MIND ABOVE

Continually walking in your freedom from sexual bondage is not a twelve-step program, or as hard as most make it. Whenever we start using approaches like those, what we are actually doing is reverting back to the law. Let's see what Paul says about this type of action in Colossians 2:23:

"Such regulations indeed have an appearance of wisdom, with their self-imposed worship, their false humility and their harsh treatment of the body, but they lack any value in restraining sensual indulgence."

Although the Apostle was talking of Jewish customs and regulations such as what to or what not to eat and the observance of special days, that scripture bears relevance to what we are talking of here. Whenever we talk of the power of the law, we are talking of human effort to please God and no one can keep all 638 laws of the old covenant. That's why Jesus came to do away with the law, so we don't have to strive to please God, but use the power of His *grace* to win. It seems logical to punish the body even today by starving it in a forty day fast, but if your mind is not converted, you'll get back into that same addiction on the 41st day after you break that fast. That's because harsh treatment of the body without God's *grace* lacks any value in restraining sensual indulgence, as the scriptures state.

Someone may ask: "So, does it mean we can now do whatever we want because as long as we are under *grace*, we can't fall again?"

Well friend, that's what the Holy Spirit was explaining to us in the first six chapters of this book (this includes me, the writer).

Now that you're free from this sexual bondage (prayerfully this is true for you reader), you have an obligation to constantly set your mind on things above where Christ is; this means a continued increase of Christ consciousness, just as Peter talked of growing in the knowledge of Christ. You won't leave your door wide open when going on a vacation, even if you have a powerful alarm system, right? Likewise, you shouldn't allow anything to run through your mind unchecked. To set your mind above, you have to die daily to your three greatest enemies which are the world, the devil, and the flesh. Satan will not leave you alone, but will continue to mount pressure and try to bring to your mind the thrills you used to have with the past addiction. When that happens, stand your ground and remember these three Fs: Faith, Flee, and Fight.

> **World** — Faith (You overcome by your faith in Christ. The victory is already won for you. – 1 John 5:4)
> **Flesh** — Flee (Run away from compromising situations that will tempt your flesh. – 2 Timothy 2:22)
> **Devil** — Fight (This is not your own power, but Christ's. Stand your ground and fight by resisting Satan constantly. – 1 Peter 5:9)

Remember, this is by the *grace* of God, so don't rely on your own strength. You'll soon find out it's so easy that you'll ask yourself why you didn't know this sooner.

I'll see you at the top of the mountains of success as we continue in this conquest for our Lord and Savior Jesus Christ.

If you've never accepted Jesus Christ as your personal Savior and Lord, or you have but turned your back on Him, please say this prayer out loud right now:

"Dear God, I want to be a part of Your family. You said in Your Word that if I acknowledge that You raised Jesus from the dead, and that I accept Him as my Lord and Savior, I would be saved. So God, I now say that I believe You raised Jesus from the dead and that He is alive and well. I accept Him now as my personal Lord and Savior. I accept my salvation from sin right now.

I am now saved. Jesus is my Lord. Jesus is my Savior. Thank you, Father God, for forgiving me, saving me, and giving me eternal life with You. Amen!"

REFERENCES

1. Wifey Wednesday: Can Christians use sex toys
   https://tolovehonorandvacuum.com/2011/11/wifey-wednesday-can-christians-use-sex-toys/
2. BAR THE GATES
   http://www.wisdomonline.org/devotionals/devotion_detail.html?id=858
3. 10 reasons David is called "a man after God's own heart."
   http://www.biblestudytools.com/blogs/ron-edmondson/10-reasons-david-is-called-a-man-after-god-s-own-heart.html
4. Uriah's wife
   http://www.1timothy4-13.com/files/proverbs/bathsheba.html
5. Most Bizzare Sexual Cultures and Practices
   http://www.therichest.com/rich-list/most-shocking/10-most-bizarre-sexual-cultures-and-practices/
6. Top 10 Effects of Porn on Your Brain, Your Marriage, and Your Sex Life
   https://tolovehonorandvacuum.com/2014/03/effects-of-porn-on-your-marriage/
7. GUARD YOUR GATES
   http://www.studyjesus.com/Religion_Library/Sermon_on_the_Mount/06_GuardGates.htm
8. REBUILDING THE WALL
   https://www.cgg.org/index.cfm/fuseaction/Library.sr/CT/PW/k/144/Rebuilding-Wall.htm
9. CNN: The changing reasons why women cheat on their husbands
   http://edition.cnn.com/2017/10/05/health/why-women-cheat-partner/index.html

10. New study shows why women have better sense of smell
https://timesofindia.indiatimes.com/home/science/New-study-shows-why-women-have-better-sense-of-smell/articleshow/45057073.cms

11. BASIC INTRODUCTION TO SOUL TIES
http://www.greatbiblestudy.com/soulties.php

About the Author

Albert Amara is a naturalized American citizen originally from Sierra Leone, West Africa. He is the author of three books: *Inspirations From Downrange*, *The Enoch Lifestyle*, and *The Due Process*. Albert and his wife Hilary are the pastors of Agape Word Embassy in Ansbach, Germany and the parents of four children.

You can connect with Albert Amara on the following media sites:

https://www.facebook.com/albert.amara.3
https://twitter.com/amaraalbert
https://www.youtube.com/channel/UCrUYov0JTN4F29rsOs TyQcQ?view_as=subscriber
amaraalbert@yahoo.com
and on Instagram @Albert Amara